THE
CHRISTIAN
AND
SOCIAL
ACTION

CHARLES Y. FURNESS

FLEMING H. REVELL COMPANY
Old Tappan, New Jersey

Scripture quotations in this volume are from the
KING JAMES VERSION of the Bible.

Library of Congress Cataloging in Publication Data

Furness, Charles Y
    The Christian and social action.

    Bibliography: p.
    1.   Church and social problems—United States.
2.   Social action.   3.   Evangelicalism.   I.   Title.
HN39.U6F9   261.8′3′0973   72-4527
ISBN 0-8007-0564-5

Contents

Preface

EVANGELICAL SOCIAL CONCERN

Within the last thirty years, a few evangelical Christians have been talking and writing about an awakening social consciousness and social concern among evangelicals.

Within the last five years, we have begun to declare, in evangelical bodies assembled, that the spiritual and social problems of the United States of America are moving us to social action where possible. Some are coming to see the parallel between the use of medical ministries and various technical, educational, and social services on the foreign mission field, along with evangelism, and the need to use such varied ministries along with the gospel here at home.

Accordingly, some evangelical denominations and interdenominational organizations are coming to consider the inner city as a home mission field. Complex and explosive social problems exist elsewhere as well as in the inner city, but inner city needs are at this time so evident that to many observers they appear high on the list of priorities for evangelical action. Examples of declarations by evangelicals about the inner city and other social concerns may be seen in the proceedings of the U.S. Congress on Evangelism, Minneapolis, September, 1969, and in the Wheaton Declaration, April, 1966.

Some evangelical workers who have been in long and constant daily contact with social problems are beginning to suggest to their fellow evangelicals how they might act on such problems. A definition of an evangelical Christian is imperative here so as to know who these evangelical workers are, and who are the evangelicals they are calling to greater involvement in helping people in need.

An evangelical Christian believes the revealed essentials of the faith delivered to the Church by the God who reveals Himself in the Scriptures. However much evangelicals may and do differ on issues on which there is no revelation, and on the interpretation of some about which there is revealed truth, they are united on basic beliefs about which there is no doubt as to their clear stipulation in the Scriptures. They may be summarized as follows:

A Christian is one who has exercised personal faith in Jesus Christ as Saviour and Lord, and trusts in Jesus' blood for cleansing from sin.[1] The message from God that this salvation is available is the evangel, the gospel, the "good news." They who believe this evangel are evangelicals.

The evangelical, as he becomes instructed in the Scriptures, sees them as the Word of God, fully and verbally inspired and inerrant in the original writings, and authoritative in matters of faith and life. While an evangelical statement of faith could include many cardinal points under it, such a list of inclusions would be headed by belief in the Deity of Jesus Christ; His conception by God the Holy Spirit; His birth through a virgin, Mary; His substitutionary sacrifice on the cross; His physical resurrection, ascension, and present living session at the right hand of God; and His physical second coming.

Such are the basic beliefs of the evangelical workers who, day in and day out, grapple with many social problems, from the simplest to the most complex. These workers are calling for positive action programs in the face of such needs.

Positive Action Programs

The first requisite in a positive program is to know what facilities are already available in church and community, and what programs are already in operation to meet human need. One of the contentions of this book is that there are forms of social action in which some Christians have been engaging and with which they are so familiar that they do not even realize they are social action. Even when we call some activity church work instead of social action, there is no need to deny that the nature of much help given by churches is social action even though called by another name.

The second requisite of such a program includes delineation of what ought yet to be done now and what might later become possible. There must be a reassessment of all means by which churches may help those who are in need—around them and within their own group. Each such evaluation should lead to action by use of these resources wherever possible.

Understanding Social Problems

It is not scripturally sound to conceive of each lone Christian as launched forth *on his own* to change society. He is a member both of the church of which he is a member and of the entire body of Christ, the Church. As such, he is an extension of the local church and one of its representatives in the community. Never before has it been so necessary for each church to be informed on social problems and how to cope with them, so as to guide each Christian in his individual testimony and influence.

The local church, where possible, in addition to instructing each new Christian in how to live the Christian life, should guide him in how he as a Christian is to understand social problems. Such understanding is for his own edification and for his fruitful service to others around him. When a person is converted to Christ he influences society beneficially. He can influence it even more to the extent to which he is given instruction in how to do so should specific situations of human need confront him.

Use of Knowledge Is Itself a Method

How is the question in the field of social action. By what methods can wrongs be righted? The *use* of knowledge is itself a method. Understanding of people and problems in which the people are involved is imperative to successful work with them. To so large a degree, understanding is based on knowledge of facts. Once gained, knowledge is combined with other components to form an effective tool.

Strategy and Tactics

God makes some social action strategies very plain in the Scriptures. Some of the tactics by which these strategies are to be implemented are also set forth there. Many tactics and substrategies should be devised by Christians. These must be in keeping with the Scriptures. Evangelical understanding of social action, of massive social problems, and of how to minister to human need, coupled with the use of evangelical Christian action, are urgently needed today.

Focus on Need

The central focus of this book is on human need and on evangelical action to meet that need. Need, once truly realized, impels action. Human needs are evidenced in present social crises and in social problems in general. Several of the areas of major importance which we consider and their relation to human need are:

The Individual and the Group

The importance of the individual and his particular life situation and relationships with others are of prime concern to God and to the Christian. Much is said in these pages about the individual, and always in relation to his needs. At the same time, the group is not belittled at the expense of the individual nor is it exalted above the individual. The group properly understood and worked with is a means of assistance to each individual in the group.

The Poor

In looking at poverty and the poor, it is our intent to focus on the needs of the poor rather than discuss how they became poor. Action to help them is imperative. Protestations against abusers of the poor are very much in order. The Scriptures inveigh frequently against those who neglect and persecute the poor.

The Black Americans

All who desire to minister to human need should understand black Americans better, and the plight of so many of them. Whatever this book says about their past and present is said to emphasize their need and to stir action to help them.

Action to help other minority groups is needed also. Poor whites, Mexican-Americans, American Indians, other poor, could as easily have been chosen for study. We single out the blacks for special mention because (1) they are a minority group very representative of all American poor, whether rural or urban; (2) they are additionally disadvantaged because of racial differences and discrimination; and (3) they have finally come to a conspicuous position in American life to which they should have come much sooner, but were prevented by racism and discrimination. More than even these reasons, we consider them because they have *needs* and are representative of so many others with identical problems.

Social Work

The profession of social work takes some of our attention for two reasons. As a helping profession it is a logical tool for use in helping people. Also, there are some social work techniques which should be employed by Christians. Along with these there are some governmental social welfare regulations and professional social work standards with which evangelicals should comply in performing some of their own social service ministries. This does not give blanket approval to all social work programs, philosophies, and personnel. In fact, we are not saying that social work is good or bad. We are simply asserting that social work provides additional channels by which Christians may help people in need.

Evangelical Christian Social Work

Within the broad purview of evangelical Christian social action there is emerging a pattern of evangelical Christian social work, or social service. Sectarian or religious social services are becoming parts of some evangelical church and church-related programs of assistance.

DEVELOPMENT OF THE TEXT, AND ACKNOWLEDGMENTS

Chapter 1 is introductory. It summarizes the subject of social action in advance, and acquaints the reader with several of the many current uses of the term "social action."

Chapters 2 through 9 comprise Part I, "Social Action Today," on popular and prominent aspects of social action now.

Chapters 10 through 21 examine some social action of the past and present and contain discussion of Christian action.

The material in this book has grown out of the author's experience in the pastorate, rescue mission administration, professional social work practice in evangelical settings, and present teaching at Philadelphia College of Bible.

The author's studies at the Theological Seminary of the Reformed Episcopal Church clarified his apologetic and crystallized his understanding of the biblical doctrine of good works, both essential for treating the material covered in this book.

Throughout the text, confidence is expressed that evangelicals do respond in the form of effective action when they are fully aware of existing conditions and led in action to correct them. Experience with evangelicals through the years, especially those of Northern New Jersey in Newark and vicinity, has indicated the wisdom of encouraging evangelicals to labor together in evangelization and Christian social service ministries in an area. Particularly is the author deeply appreciative of encouragement in study and research shown him by the Board of Trustees of the Goodwill Home and Rescue Mission, Newark, New Jersey. Beginning in 1962, having to write down parts of this book's material for a variety of articles and lectures led to the writing of this manuscript. Then followed adaptations from two sets of special lecture notes by the author. These were in connection with the Christian Thought and Ministry Lectureship at Conservative Baptist Theological Seminary, Denver, Colorado, October, 1966, and the 1967 Bueermann-Champion Lectureship at the Western Conservative Baptist Theological Seminary, Portland, Oregon, September, 1967.

I greatly appreciate the courtesies extended me by several of my colleagues of Philadelphia College of Bible. Faculty members John W. Cawood, Renald E. Showers, and Ralph W. Eckardt, Jr., read this manuscript, especially from the standpoints of their disciplines. Benjamin W. Johnson read the manuscript as a close associate in inner city ministries. Other College-connected friends gave valuable comments.

My deepest gratitude is due to Dr. Frank E. Gaebelein and Dr. David O. Moberg for reading the manuscript and giving generously of their comments and encouragement.

Particular thanks are due to my wife, Margaret S. Furness, and to Marjorie E. Phillips, especially for help in gathering my material and preparation of the first draft.

Charles Y. Furness

Reference for the Preface
1. 1 John 1:7.

Acknowledgments

The author appreciates permission granted for use of the following material:

Quotation from pages 467 and 469 from *Sociology of Social Problems* by Paul B. Horton and Gerald R. Leslie. Copyright © (1965) 1970. Used by permission of Appleton-Century-Crofts, Educational Division, Meredith Corporation.

Quotations from pages 3, 122, 123, 126 and 130 from Robert G. Clouse, Robert D. Linder and Richard V. Pierard (eds.), *Protest and Politics* (Greenwood, S.C., The Attic Press, 1968). Used by permission of The Attic Press, Inc., copyright holder.

Quotation as follows: From Special Introduction by Tom Wicker to the *Report of the National Advisory Commission on Civil Disorders*. Copyright © 1968 by the New York Times Company. Used by permission of Bantam Books, Inc. (p. vii).

Quotation from pages 10 and 11, Richard Hofstadter, *Social Darwinism in American Thought* (Boston, The Beacon Press, revised, paperback, 1955). Copyright 1944, 1955 by the American Historical Association and is reprinted by permission of Beacon Press.

Quotation from J. A. Witmer, "Christian Social Responsibility," *Bibliotheca Sacra*, vol. 10, no. 437 (January, 1953), pages 218, 219, used by permission.

Quotations from Billy Graham, *World Aflame* (New York, Doubleday and Co., 1965), pages 182, 184. Copyright © by Billy Graham, 1965, and used by permission.

Quotations from James O. Buswell, III, *Slavery, Segregation and the Scriptures* (Grand Rapids, Wm. B. Eerdmans Publishing Co., 1954), pages 34, 35; and Carl F. H. Henry, *The Uneasy Conscience of Modern Fundamentalism* (Grand Rapids, Wm. B. Eerdmans Publishing Co., 1954), pages 30, 32, 39 and 80. Used by permission.

Quotations from pages 455, 456 from *The Human Group* by George C. Homans, copyright, 1950, by Harcourt Brace Jovanovich, Inc., and are reprinted with their permission.

Quotations from Harvey Cox, *The Secular City* (New York, The Macmillan Co., paperback, 1965), page 110. Copyright © Harvey Cox, 1965, 1966. Used by permission.

THE CHRISTIAN AND SOCIAL ACTION

1

Introduction: The Christian and Social Crises

"Social Action" Means Many Things

A radio voice at commercial time once asked a question: "Wouldn't you like to do volunteer work for a social action organization?"

Another recent advertisement for a nationally known civic organization suggested that joining it and making special contributions through it was "social action."

On the occasion of seeing television pictures of the first astronaut landing on the moon, an eleven-year-old boy was heard to remark that he didn't want to go to the moon because there was no action there, no playmates. He was concerned with social interaction, which is basic to many human relationships, including social action.

These are a few of several ways in which social action may be understood. Not many years ago, volunteers would have been solicited for community service projects or, long ago, for charity work. Social workers who have been professionally trained know that the social work profession was born during a period of social reform, and that social action has been a regular part of social work process ever since. In fact, one of the important concerns of the profession today is that of determining what social action to endorse and what not to endorse.

The Christian and Social Action

What is the Christian's relationship to social action today? This is a question which an alert Christian cannot fail to consider carefully.

What should the Christian do about social action, once he understands it? Should he take any part in social action? If so, what part, in what kinds of social action, and when? How is any social action in which he might engage related to his understanding of God? To his understanding of the field of Christian service to mankind?

It is historically demonstrable that evangelical Christians have been active in social reform through the centuries, including the recent past and the present day. How shall they understand their duties and opportunities in the present context of history?

The evangelical today is being criticized for not having taken part conspicuously in the recent past in the correction of social ills. This is true to a large extent, although many of us have combated them in humble and unheralded ways. The question might well be asked, Have *any* people helped others in need as much as they should have done? The evangelical's nonparticipation was often because he did not know what action was possible; he did not have adequate leadership and training even if he did know; and he often did not realize how greatly needed he was.

How the evangelical got out of the main arena in which he worked with evangelicals and nonevangelicals alike in combating social problems of common community concern is a story to be partly reviewed in these pages. For the present we can only notice that he is expected back in action, if he is to back up his claim of being concerned about people in need.

Action is possible, and the evangelical is becoming aware of it. If he does not take action now, when he knows it to be possible and necessary, he can now be blamed. He cannot and must not fail to act when he knows what action to take and how to take it.

The Christian and the Community

A generation ago and before, the people in the community around a church to a large extent would not expect such an institution to involve itself in the community life around it if it did not wish to do so. If a church did not wish to do so, it was either because the people comprising its membership no longer lived in the vicinity and traveled to it once or twice a week, or the congregation was of a type to keep itself aloof for social and even religious reasons.

Since World War II, changes have taken place in many community expectations and attitudes. In very many instances, the relationships of church and community are much as described above. Most significant is the growing number of instances in which a church is subject to curiosity if not scrutiny or even investigation by the community around it. If the church in question is not constructively active in the community, it is tacitly if not explicitly challenged to explain why it has any reason to be located in the community.

What is the announced purpose of each church? Can it be true to its evangelistic purpose and engage in community action? In the face of human need manifested in the community around it, does a church go beyond the bounds of its prescribed functions in addressing itself to such need? Can all churches be considered likely to be helpful, or only some churches? Some church bodies may declare themselves to be obligated to help with community problems, others may feel sincerely that they are only minimally responsible.

Granted that a church wants to be of help, what problems are involved in collaboration with the community? Does that church always assume either that the community does or does not want the church to be of help to it? It is self-evident that the community may not always want what the church can supply or want it in the way the church wants to give it. As we might expect, the offense and reproach of Christ and His cross are very real factors in some such situations.[1]

Giving proper weight to these realities, can we not at the same time see the opportunity, the challenge, of the present situation? We have been waiting, praying, working, many times in futile efforts, to reach the community. Now, at least in some ways, some communities want to establish liaison. This very fact is enough to indicate immediate action by evangelicals. This is why the Church and its colleges and seminaries must train pastors and laymen to know how to work with the community in meeting community needs, and how to preserve and present its own evangelical message at the same time.

The Church at this present point in history should assert clearly one of Jesus' pronouncements. He stated that His kingdom is "not of this world." [2] This does not mean that His followers are not to concern themselves with alleviating the distresses of their fellow men. It does mean that the attitude and perspective of the Christian should be patterned after that of our Lord. He kept Himself aloof from involvement in some social issues and threw Himself into denunciation of and correction of some other conditions. A word by Sherwood Eliot Wirt on proper perspective is in order here: "Our Lord's primary interest was not the shoring up of a sagging social structure, but the ushering in of an altogether new order . . . that imminent event could not help but affect his attitude toward some of the social issues of the day." [3] Because our perspective includes the eventual triumph of the King of kings and a belief that He is at work in the world today, we have true interest in the social issues of the day and the part we may have in coming to grips with them. As He works through us in advance of His coming victory, we know we are to be of service to mankind as His representatives.

It is evident that social issues have theological connotations. Nothing social is truly understood except as it is seen to be one part of God's dealings with His creatures and His regulation of interaction among them. Wirt says, "The early Hebrews learned at the foot of Mount Sinai that in the sight of God there is indeed a difference between the sacred and the profane, but there is no difference between the spiritual and the social. Social wrongs, to God, are moral wrongs." [4] While the denotation put upon the word social in some contexts would cause a difficulty here, we can say that in the generic sense in which they are used in this reference, the use of spiritual and social is parallel to the way we should equate theological and social.

If there is any puzzle in anyone's mind about how social and spiritual elements are associated together, such a person should realize that this is not any greater an issue than that of understanding how God who is a Spirit could create a material world, or how Jesus could have both Divine and human natures and be completely both Divine and human and not merely half Divine and half human. Such matters do not defy reason; they transcend reason. This same principle holds true for the social and spiritual sides of moral issues.

Today's Idea of Social Action

Social action is associated these days with efforts to change existing methods and conditions of social relationships or to bring about some changes which have not existed before. Such efforts are usually outside customary social change channels. Some such efforts are composed of permissible change processes which have not been used often recently or in the forms they take today.

Some of these efforts are being tested by their users as to their effectiveness and their permissibility. These may range from parades and strikes to planned or spontaneous violence.

There are varying degrees of favorable or unfavorable reactions to social action as it is usually construed today. The kind of reaction to social action depends upon who initiates it or is the recipient of the action and who observes and criticizes it.

Social action in the popular sense of the term has often come to smack of drastic action, disruption of status quos, confrontation of established institutions and procedures with demanded changes, demonstrations, riots, revolution. Yet social action may be some or none of these things and bring about beneficial change. It is the threat of harmful change that causes concern. The question is, is the threat harmful only because changes that should be made are feared, or is it harmful because conditions which should continue are threatened?

For a Christian to live in these times and not have a feeling of responsibility for helping people who are in need is an indication that such a Christian has not yet come to understand the Scriptures on his social responsibility. This is not to say that the Christian is to acquiesce to all that is done in the name of social action. Far from it. It *is* to say that each Christian ought to realize his key position as a representative of God's action in the world. As he does this, he familiarizes himself with social action issues and asks God to lead him in what he should do or not do. He determines his course of action in accordance with the Scriptures and by the leading of the Holy Spirit.

Christian Social Action

It is to be expected that evangelical Christians will object to social action extremes, such as riots, and any demonstrations the leadership or execution of which have no constructive purpose or moral justification, as shall be seen later in this study.

Object to extremes we ought. Yet the problem persists: What are *we* doing about the problems which others go about to solve, whether or not we like their methods? How do we sort out legitimate and urgent needs people have? How do we go about helping them in ways that get the job done efficiently for them, acceptably to God and in conformity with existing laws and regulations? In some instances, how do we succeed in getting the laws changed if change is needed to be of true service to them?

Christians certainly recognize that changes are often needed in solving social problems. Change and conflict seem so closely associated in the minds of social action advocates today. Do we have to assume that there must be conflict among men, polarizations, confrontations, to bring about change?

Dr. Daniel Thursz says, "No one denies that in many instances contact and communication will help resolve community problems. But to argue that there is a mutuality of interests between rich and poor, landlord and slumdweller, employed and jobless, suburbanite and inner city inhabitant, welfare worker and client, farmer and migrant is to deny the existence of some fundamental differences, conflicts of interests, and unequal power distribution." [5]

The Christian does not deny the existence of inequalities and conflicts. He tries to understand when social injustices drive some groups to cause conflict in order to get redress and improvement of conditions. He needs to know what problems people have, what sources of help are available to them, what recourse to law they have.

The evangelical understands that social conflict is a sociological and psychological fact within society caused by differences among men. He also knows that all men have sinned against God [6] and that some differences among men start up because basic conflicts stem from man's sinful nature.

What Planned Social Action Is

Social action is best understood when each social act comprising it is analyzed, each cause of each act understood, and responsibility for each act determined. Using this procedure in planning any social action before it is carried out might well prevent ill-advised and unjustified action.

A long-familiar side of social action comes into view when we consider undesirable changes or deviations in the normal social functioning of society. Deviation stirs action by members of society, activity which may be referred to as social action. In the broad sense of the term, this is planned social action.

If deviant, delinquent, criminal, or psychopathic behavior persists, society organizes more formally to restore the normal condition and to attempt rehabilitation of those causing the difficulty.

Communities take steps of this kind through both governmental and private social agencies as well as through all other available community facilities. The process is somewhat as follows: The involved agency representatives survey the problems and needs causing the crisis, and study the people connected with and affected by the problems and needs. Plans are made to deal with the issues, and goals are set. Referred to more formally on larger scales of operation, these are referred to as social planning and social goals. All that remains is to adopt policies by which the plans will be carried out and then to carry them out, to *act*. This is and always has been referred to in social welfare circles as *social action*.

The social action is the result of working out the problems. *Working out* a problem includes both the planning and the action resulting from the planning.

Community action to deal with social problems is more structured than social reform and social revolution in those instances in which the latter take place by sheer force of events without deliberate human planning. God often influences men to change social conditions by community action in problem solving. While it should be kept in mind that He often chooses to change society by the operation of His special grace in spiritual awakenings and their resultant social reforms, He also works less spectacularly by His common grace through efficient functioning of social institutions, including deliberate action taken to improve conditions.

Community action on social problems is one instance of God's bringing about His purposes in society. This is one reason why evangelicals ought to master methods of social action and know which ones to use as long as they do not violate Christian principles. Concentration must be upon helping to meet human need, using whatever methods are indicated in the context of each need. If those in the world around us see genuine concern on our part for human woes, they are more likely to give ear to the Eternal Message we have for them. Even if they do not heed the gospel, they cannot accuse us of neglect of social responsibility if we help when we can.

Some Connected Observations

We have already said that social action, including evangelical Christian social action, is imperative today to avert catastrophe and disaster. This is a deliberate emphasis at this point in our discussion. It is a necessary emphasis even though revolutionary ideologies and extreme action sooner or later become dulled and merge into the existing social order after changing it somewhat, or sometimes not at all.[7] The Christian knows there are many extremes he cannot oppose because he has not the power, the opportunity, nor the clear leading of the Lord to do so. When he does have all these, he ought not hesitate to work in the direction of constructive and ameliorative change. He must be alert to this responsibility, because violent intergroup conflict for now seems more likely to accelerate than to subside in the opposite direction of peaceful accord.

Although we might wrestle simultaneously with the spiritual problems and the social problems, we must be clear on one thing in particular. Evangelism and social action must not be confused with one another. One must be sure of what each of these really is. Each is to be done separately as opportunity is afforded—under evangelical auspices, or at other times a Christian may be called upon individually to engage in social action and to evangelize at the same time. This does not combine social action and evangelism except in the collateral use of them. Wirt pens a timely caution: "When social action is mistaken for evangelism the church has ceased to manufacture its own blood cells and is dying of leukemia. When social action becomes more important than evangelism the church has forgotten to breathe and is already dead of heart failure."[8]

In the midst of agitation for social action, the Christian must beware of the misconception that these social problems now besetting us are new ones. They are old problems often manifested in new forms and combinations, but basically the same, nonetheless. Problems like poverty and racial strife are centuries old, in this country as well as elsewhere.

Systems Change

Drastic action against existing political and economic institutions to the extremes seen in riots and insurrection in recent years is action that speaks volumes. While riots as such are not justifiable, they cannot always be passed off as completely without value. When they are eruptions of intolerable human suffering, they tell us that there are underlying conditions that need attention. They may tell us that there are parts of our economic system that do not provide for the needs of the poor and do not effectuate the delivery of vital human services to them. To that degree, they tell us that parts of our social system need adjustment.

Sociologists today are in the vanguard of those who are clamoring for *systems change*. They call for changes in the political, economic, and other social systems which are imperative [9] so as to provide better delivery of services to the poor and to initiate adequate supply of services where none exist as yet. Such changes should take place by appropriate use of existing machinery. If they do not, the pressure of extreme need will force them to take place by unusual means, perhaps by violence.

Agitation incited by purposeful disrupters and which capitalizes on the extreme frustration and deprivation of the poor is one thing. Quite another thing is the aroused indignation of people living long in disadvantagement and going unheeded as they remonstrate against inequities. The removal of inadequacies and the replacement of them with supplies for better living will go far to meet the legitimate needs of the multitudes who do not have many of even the bare necessities of life.

References for Chapter 1
1. Hebrews 11:26; 13:13.
2. John 18:36.
3. Sherwood E. Wirt, *The Social Conscience of the Evangelical* (New York, Harper and Row, 1968), p. 24.
4. *Ibid.*, pp. 9, 10.
5. Daniel Thursz, "Social Action as a Professional Responsibility," *Social Work*, Vol. 11, No. 3 (July, 1966), p. 14.

6. Psalms 14:1–3; Romans 3:9–26.
7. See Peter L. Berger, *Invitation to Sociology* (Garden City, Double-day and Co., Anchor Books, 1963), p. 47.
8. Wirt, *op. cit.*, p. 129.
9. Health and Welfare Council, Philadelphia, Pa., "Guidelines for Action," *Advance*, Newsletter of the Council, Vol. 7, No. 2 (November–December, 1969), p. 1.

PART I

Social Action Today

2

The Plight of the Blacks

Overview of the American Negro Experience

Many of the blacks in our country are in a predicament. Some of this condition is traceable to the slavery they experienced in their earlier history in America. Their plight stems also from other forms of denial of opportunity and from discrimination during three hundred fifty years' disadvantagement experienced by most American blacks.

Another complication is that to which Robert D. Linder refers as "a kind of traditional mass indifference on the part of great numbers of Protestants to the plight of many Americans wallowing in the mire of second-class citizenship." [1]

To these factors of oppression and indifference must be added that of widespread ignorance of the facts. Many middle- and upper-class Americans simply do not know the realities of living in ascribed inferiority.

It is not our intention to berate today's white Americans for the actions of their forefathers. Slavery or inferiority of blacks or other minority groups appeared as normal social facts to many of them. As Linder says, Christianity was often accommodated to the institution of slavery rather than the institution being destroyed by Christian values. [2] Our forebears are not around to absorb any berating we might do. It is rather of infinitely greater importance that *today's* white Americans face and correct today's discrimination and indifference.

No man should be considered to be inferior nor should he be treated so. Also, whites and nonwhites in unison must agree that equality and opportunity should be the experience of all Americans *NOW*.

The Plight of the Black Poor and Other Poor

In speaking of Negro needs, our intention is to point out the needs of all poor people of whatever group. However minority groups may differ from one another otherwise, poverty gives them a large base of common identity. Likewise the white poor, themselves a minority group within the white majority in America, have common cause with the other poor.

With no intention to neglect notice of the needs of Mexican-American, Puerto Rican, other Latin-American, American Indian, poor white, and other minorities, it is timely that we examine the Negroes as a representative minority. Examine we should as long as we do something about their needs if we can. Action by evangelicals when God makes it possible is desirable on the basis that we represent the Lord Jesus in ministering to the needs of our neighbors.

While making some mention of inner city violence, it is important that we do not dismiss major riots as merely race riots. Race riots are serious enough in themselves. In our country, there have been all too many race riots in the past three hundred years. Serious as the racial aspect of recent riots is, it is only a major *part* of the basis for present upheaval on the part of so many of our nation's poor.

Sketch of Recent Black American Experience

At various points in our study we will be looking at developments in the long history of the black Americans, but only enough to apply each such reference to a present situation, to help understand the present problems of the blacks.

One such development is migrations whenever and however possible from the South to the North, whether from slavery to freedom or from rural deprivation to beckoning city opportunity. Two major migrations were during the last quarter of the nineteenth century and during World War I.[3]

The predicament of today's Negro was compounded in this century as he came out of the South in response to a demand for laborers. This crisis period developed further, after World War II, as blacks saw opportunities outside the Old South. It progressed in the upsurge of American blacks, along with others of the world's nonwhite population. It climaxed as American Negro leaders emerged in the black advance of the 1960s.

The United States Supreme Court action in 1954, in desegregating the schools, marked the beginning of several outward evidences of the showing of real concern for the Negro plight on the part of governmental leadership. With boycotts and sit-ins climaxed by freedom rides and events like the 1963 March on Washington and passing of the 1964 Civil Rights legislation, it seemed that Negro emancipation was at last sanctioned as government responded to pressure. It seemed as if all that were needed, for all people and situations, was to fall in line with both letter and spirit of the law and adjust progress and performance to the new mood. Naive, yes—optimistic, true; to the uninitiated layman, a plausible thought.

The 1964 Civil Rights Act seemed to be the one major action

that could dispel likelihood of revolution. It may have actually done so. There was near-revolution in the days of the Great Depression, in the opinion of some of us who witnessed trends of that time. There were and are worse unemployment conditions since that time in present poverty areas. There is often a two and three times greater rate of unemployment in Negro ghetto areas today than in the entire nation during the Depression. Our national leaders took strong measures in the mid-sixties to stave off great upheavals. While the 1964 Civil Rights Act did not directly alleviate the conditions of unemployment of minority group members to any great or immediate extent, it so enhanced recognition of Negro equality that major threats of violence seemed minimized.

Gravity of the Lack of Minimally Satisfactory Living Conditions

Why did violence erupt more vehemently in 1967 than it did before 1964, in the face of evidence that our Government had recognized needs of the minority groups and the poor by civil rights and antipoverty legislation? Surely, some observers might reason, crises seldom develop into revolutionary proportions. Especially are they slow to develop to that point if rulers are sincere in wanting to change conditions for the better and accordingly take action to bring about such change.

Prevailing conditions are much too complex for such an over-simplification. Failure of the expected result of greater change brought about by the legislation could mean only one thing: There are conditions present in our society so serious and extensive that even gestures of the magnitude of Supreme Court decisions could not avail if they do not eliminate and change these conditions extensively and soon enough.

Ignorance of adverse living conditions and failure to realize that these conditions cause desperation are all too common among those who do not know the disadvantaged lives of our nation's poor. They are suffering from many lacks and abuses of which the main problems are unemployment, poor education, poor housing, and poor health. It also cannot be denied that many suffering in these ways will never be otherwise because improvements cannot be made soon enough.

It is also true that the poor are aware that their plight gets steadily worse. With so many other people farther up on the stratification ladder and rising farther, the poor are increasingly worse off than before merely by holding their own. With the rising costs of living and higher taxes they are really not holding their own economically.

What has just been noted about the poor in general is equally true of the black poor. In a number of instances the Negroes are even worse off than the others. This is due to the prejudice and discrimination they suffer and the lack of opportunity to advance so often true in their experience.

In spite of some militant exceptions, the Negroes are for the most part as friendly and patient as other people (and the other people have militant exceptions, too!). They are usually willing to cooperate if others in good faith collaborate with them to improve their lot. This is remarkable in the face of what they have gone through. They have given us perhaps the greatest object lesson in American history of what flesh and blood can endure at the hands of other humans and still have any identity or potential left. The only parallel, on a world-wide scale, has been that of the Jews. The Jews suffered so extremely through the centuries, and especially in World War II. Yet even the Jews, outbursts and attitudes of anti-Semitism in America notwithstanding, did not in the United States suffer the deprivation and disadvantagement experienced by the American Negroes.

The prospect of being increasingly less likely to emerge from poverty has galvanized blacks to action to escape exclusion from opportunity. Negroes would not be threatening or carrying out violence and near-violence in social action efforts today if major economic hardship were not increasingly their experience. If their purchasing power were not diminishing, if they could have equal chances in employment and in housing in fact as well as in promise, and if they could have adequate educational and health facilities, they would be exerting only the normal pressures of any special interest group. They would press for more of a voice in improving their lives and would be glad to know other people were aware of their needs and planning to do something about them.

To know that Negroes are disadvantaged and on so vast a scale but do nothing about it is to contribute more injustice to the many acts of injustice already known. Whitney M. Young, Jr., former executive director of the National Urban League, remarked, "Civil rights demonstrations would be minimized, if not eliminated, if there were as much concern and indignation about the injustices and the discrimination against Negro citizens as there is about the demonstrations themselves." [4]

Spiritual Needs of the Negroes

Why do evangelicals need to know about the plight of the blacks? Their spiritual needs must be met. Just as it is necessary to know the needs of people of any kind in order to minister to them and evangelize them, the obligation is no more and no less applicable in the case of the blacks.

The Negroes are for the most part unevangelized. So many of them are religious, it is true, but they have not been too well acquainted with evangelicals and the gospel. Evangelicals often have not considered blacks as equals, or at least as socially acceptable. The blacks have felt excluded and even exploited by so many people, and many evangelicals have not been any different in their dealings with them. If only the blacks could see past the messengers to the message of the gospel itself, they would encounter a message that is not harmful, but helpful. It is literally good news, glad tidings.[5] It is imperative that those who carry the message see that stumbling blocks in their own lives and methods of ministry be removed so as not to hinder the gospel.

Negro churches are in many instances more like all-purpose centers for the congregations than the more nearly single-purpose churches of many of the whites. Admittedly, this is a generalization to which there are many exceptions, but real enough to be seen to some degree. This characteristic was caused mainly by the segregation or exclusion of blacks by whites from social, religious, political, economic, and educational gathering places and programs.

Many Negro churches, like many nonblack ones, discarded the gospel message. They continued only as social gathering places, preaching messages which did not include the gospel. When this happens to churches, black and white alike, they need evangelizing.

Evangelicals have gone to great lengths to evangelize Negroes in Africa, the West Indies, South America, and elsewhere. At least in recent years the evangelicals for the most part have not sought to evangelize American blacks, except occasionally as they came across their paths. This was largely because it was taken for granted that the Negro churches would evangelize their own people. It is certainly an evidence of God's love for His people in that God used many of the Negroes to do that very thing. Had it not been for faithful blacks pointing many

more to Christ, we would not have the many black evangelicals
ready for the present challenge of evangelism.

Religious Aspects of Civil Disorders

The report of two organizations, Urban America, Inc., and
the Urban Coalition, covered in the public press of February 27,
1969,[6] reminds us of a prior report issued a year earlier. The
more recent report says that the warning of the previous report,
the National Advisory Commission on Civil Disorders *Report*,
had not been heeded to any great extent in the intervening year.
Because recommended action was not taken, the nation was seen
according to the later report to be continuing to drift toward
what the Commission had called, "two societies, one black, one
white—separate and unequal." [7]

The Advisory Commission *Report* has been criticized for political and economic content not pleasing to some readers. Criticisms notwithstanding, it has proven a monumental depiction of
the stark reality that has changed very little since it was written.
For purposes of studying inner city and ghetto conditions and accompanying social problems it is a valuable source book, and will
long remain so.

The Commission *Report* says nothing in any systematic way
about the role of religion in riot areas. However, the perceptive
evangelical cannot miss a most evident fact revealed in the descriptions of disorder. This is the *sin* of man, white and black
man alike. The fact of man's sinful nature was a theological
reality observable as it affected antagonists in the riots, whatever
their race or other identity. The heart of man is more significant
than his pigmentation, a fact never more vividly illustrated than
in these instances. Vivid examples of conduct during civil disorders which expose the sin of man [8] are certainly clear enough
to convince the evangelical observer that he must want to do

something about such spiritual ills should he have a chance to do so.

We must rest assured that if we do not trouble ourselves to fight many of the social ills which afflict our fellow Americans, they will not be too interested in what we profess to want to do for their spiritual needs.

Is it too late? Is it not true that many blacks identify the gospel with white people? Bringing the gospel into disrepute in the eyes of the blacks because of conduct by the whites contradicts what might be expected of followers of Christ. Have we not obscured the gospel because we have so often failed to take the gospel to the American blacks? Have not some professing Christian whites hindered the gospel by subjugating and abusing the blacks?

It is never too late when it is God's time to act. Evangelicals both black and white must wait upon God for direction and must use both old and new methods in which they do not obstruct the gospel. God wants us first to be purged of racial prejudice, and then to take action as He leads.

Tom Wicker of the *New York Times,* when writing an Introduction to the *Report* of the National Commission on Civil Disorders, refers to the "insidious and pervasive white sense of the inferiority of black men." [9] There *are* many whites who feel this way toward blacks. It is also true that there are all too many whites, even evangelical whites, whose latent prejudice is accompanied by an active and patent prejudice. Racial prejudice is a cancer in any society. In a Christian society, it is both anomaly and sin.

Mr. Wicker is too inclusive, however, when he implies that *all* whites have such a "sense of the inferiority of black men." Blacks who assume this are also on shaky ground. No person understanding the Bible and the evangelical insistence on racial tolerance can call any human being inferior to another. There are many white Christians, thus far too inarticulate, who cannot tolerate such insinuations to the effect that *all* whites believe blacks to be inferior. There are also many Christian blacks who do not fall into a black racist category. It is quite likely that Mr. Wicker did not mean to imply that there were no exceptions to his generalization, but there are most likely many more exceptions than he might think.

(While thinking of whites considering blacks inferior, and vice versa, notice should be taken of God's rebuke to Peter for his regarding the Gentiles as inferior because they were not of the Jews.) [10]

Not only are blacks not inferior but they are equal with people of other races; they also have the same wonderful potentials God put into all men.

Given equal opportunity of employment, education, health care and living standards and conditions, and equal socialization and integration into society, blacks are proven no less and no more able to do well in all fields than members of any and all races. What has been said with regard to the Negro is true with regard to the Asiatic, the American Indian, the Mexican-American, the Puerto Rican, or any other minority group person. (God sees no one a member of a majority or a minority group. Our finite limitations force us to use such convenient terms.)

Closely related to equality is the desire of the minority group member to have *identity*. He wants to be thought of as being every bit as much a person as anyone else.

Again we use the Negroes as a case in point. They are an example of this longing of which we speak: What blacks want in particular is a sense of identity. Too long they have been thought of as inferior, as less than equal, as animals, as slaves, as property, as a group apart. The time has long since been upon us and is particularly urgent now in which the black person wants to be reckoned with as a man. He does not want himself to be thought of as less than a man, nor as an inferior man, but as a man equal with other men.

The black pressures for courses in African history and in American black history are a symptom reflecting the move toward establishing and experiencing black identity. Occasionally some observer will say that black studies will not do the blacks any good, and that what they need is concentration on *useful* subjects. It would seem that such an observer never had any need to establish his own identity. He is also forgetting, if he ever knew, that minority groups stay together for identity's sake as well as for other reasons. If this development is appreciated properly, it should in the long run aid the blacks in their moving into more areas of American life without feelings on their part or the part of others that they cannot hold up their own end of the common responsibility for American life and work. The study of black history and related subjects, properly and effectively undertaken, should help whites understand *themselves* better, as it would help blacks with their own self-awareness.

The insistence by some Negroes on being called *black* is another instance of the establishment of identity. It is a reaction against derogatory connotation of the word *Negro* which is equivalent to *slave* in the ears of some blacks. He is an equal black man rather than a Negro inferior. A trend among some black organizers is featuring African cultural revival, African history, and African dress, with some advocacy of the term "Afro-American" as a designation applied to everything that is black American.

Even discussion about intermarriage between whites and blacks is, in many cases, not an outright proposal to campaign in favor of miscegenation. It is rather part of the same insistence that a Negro be accepted as a *man,* able to do what any other man can do. He is thus not merely a Negro male—but a man first—then black. The blacks prefer to stay with their own kind in a closeness of relationship made more cohesive during the days of slavery and second-class citizenship. They do not want to be considered as seeking permission to intrude racially, sexually, economically. Seeking permission to intrude would imply that they were not entitled to participation to begin with. What they want is freedom to function within the equality that is rightfully theirs. They want to be allowed to stay to themselves by choice and not have their staying together enforced by imposed segregation policies. They also want to have the companion freedom of functioning among people different from themselves, and in all areas of life experiences as they may have opportunity and choose to do so.

References for Chapter 2

1. Robert D. Linder, "A Christian Approach to the Contemporary Civil Rights Movement," in Robert G. Clouse, Robert D. Linder and Richard V. Pierard, *Protest and Politics* (Greenwood, S.C., The Attic Press, 1968), p. 130.
2. *Ibid.,* p. 125.
3. John Hope Franklin, *From Slavery to Freedom* (New York, Vintage, 1967), pp. 399, 471–474.
4. Whitney M. Young, *To Be Equal* (New York, McGraw-Hill Book Co., 1964), p. 241.
5. Luke 2:10, 11.
6. See article by Lawrence M. O'Rourke, "2 Panels Say Gulf Between Races Is Wider," *Philadelphia Evening Bulletin* (February 27, 1969), pp. 1, 22.
7. National Advisory Commission on Civil Disorders, *Report* (New York, Bantam Books, 1968), p. 1.
8. *Ibid.,* pp. 64, 91–93.
9. *Ibid.,* p. vii.
10. Acts 10:9–28.

3

The Ghetto and the Inner City

The Ghetto

Instead of taking a broader look at urban conditions in general, we shall take particular notice of the ghetto and the inner city. Major outbreaks of violence in America through the years have been by no means restricted to city areas, but most major outbreaks recently have taken place in the cities, especially the inner city. This does not mean that these areas are qualitatively worse than anywhere else in the city or out of it. It does give some indication of the concentration of large numbers of people and the proliferation and variety of social problems occurring there.

The crowded quarters of the ghetto and accompanying social problems give many of the ghetto poor an intensified sense of being hemmed in. There seems to be a feeling on their part of permanent disadvantagement, of being consigned to a limbo of endless rejection. Of course, in no section of a city will all people affected share such a feeling consciously except under the most adverse and revolting conditions.

It is hard for the poor to stifle such feelings. Resentment seeks an outlet in physical violence. This is not to justify the violence, but to explain it. All too often it is thought to be easier to punish the violence rather than to remove the causes of it. It may be easier at the time, perhaps, but in the long run it is actually more costly in many ways. The pattern for improvement should include *both* justice *and* better living conditions, rather than *either* one *or* the other.

Also strong in the ghetto is a sense of frustration. The *Report* of the National Advisory Commission on Civil Disorders tells of the poor, Negro and otherwise, who feel increasingly a sense of being unable to hold their own. They feel they cannot qualify for jobs that would help them rise above the poverty level. Part of their frustrations grow out of their awareness of the shortcomings of local governments. A few excerpts from the *Report* reflect these and related conditions:

Municipal officials . . . appeared not to realize the volatile frustrations of Negroes in the ghetto.[1]

They were bitter about their inability to get the city government to correct conditions . . . Garbage sometimes was not picked up for two weeks in succession. Overflowing garbage cans littered streets, and cluttered empty lots were breeding grounds for rats. Inadequate storm drains led to flooded streets.[2]

Grievances . . . result from . . . powerlessness which Negroes often experience.[3]

. . . Most middle-class Americans have little comprehension of the sense of insecurity that characterizes the ghetto resident.[4]

The plight of the ghetto youth is overwhelming. Should he desire to do so, he usually cannot get out of his environment. His father is often not in the home. Crime, violence, poor housing, dope, the school drop-out experience, gang pressures, difficulty of getting a job, and practical impossibility of getting work that would result in significant economic advantage—these are his heritage and surroundings.

These conditions are not new. They have existed in some form and to some degree in American slums for nearly two centuries and have affected our poor, black or otherwise. They are intensified by increased varieties and combinations of these conditions, by additional ways of doing wrong, and by increases in population compounded by worse overcrowding.

If only all nonghetto Christians could understand these conditions, they would realize how binding it is upon us to do unto the ghetto dweller what we would want him to do for us [5] were we in the same circumstances.

So often, however, we are not informed by those who should be informing us. With the Commission *Report's* observation on the need to cover civil disorders better,[6] there will probably be an improvement in particulars of such coverage, and we can look for even better service than ever from our alert media of communication.

Once we have been informed of ghetto predicaments, the community at large, including evangelical Christians, can (1) help in any way possible to improve ghetto living conditions; (2) help facilitate living and working outside the ghetto for many at present in the ghetto; and (3) exert all influence toward development of a *single* society. The Commission *Report* says, "The primary goal must be a single society, in which every citizen will be free to live and work according to his capabilities and desires, not his color." [7]

The Ghetto Defined

What is a ghetto?

The study of the word itself is interesting, as is the development of ghettos in several parts of the world through the centuries.

For our purposes we shall use one definition of a ghetto, which we can use to give us a first glimpse of one.

A ghetto is "an area within a city characterized by poverty and acute social disorganization, and inhabited by members of a racial or ethnic group under conditions of involuntary segregation." [8]

In the version of the ghetto seen in the United States of America in the nineteen sixties and seventies, it is in most instances a concentration of people as a result of the process of modern urbanization. Racial and ethnic groups comprising them have been absorbed within the urban unit of which they are a part, but not well enough assimilated to provide a sense of well-being to ghetto residents without their seeking people similar to themselves to live in one locale with them. Therefore, we can assume that ghetto formation often is partly by preference. In many, perhaps most, large American cities, the word *involuntary* in the definition given above is appropriate, once the ghetto is established.

How many nonghetto residents have ever been in a ghetto?

There are exceptions and bright spots in contrast to the prevailing conditions a visitor to the ghetto might see, but the ghetto scene is much like this:

Rats. Roaches. Garbage and other debris in great quantity randomly scattered outside and very often within many of the dwellings. Too often a one-room, or two-room, "home" for two, five, eight, eleven people. Little or no personal privacy with little or no concept of what privacy can be. Mail very often tampered with. Expectation of physical battle to keep personal property. Intrusions by neighbors, transients, imminent if not usual. Domination by gang influences. Exploitation and manipulation by criminals or unscrupulous business interests. Hunger. Malnutrition. Disease. Poor schools. Joblessness. Filth. Stenches.

The injustice is that most residents do not want it this way! Since most of them know nothing better, they have to put up with it and even accommodate themselves to it in a somewhat accepting way. Even so, they vaguely wish conditions were better.

Too many people who are not acquainted firsthand with what goes together to create ghetto conditions are likely to say something like, "Those people don't live much better than animals, anyway. You can take the people out of the ghetto and put them in better housing but you can't take the ghetto out of the people. Whether they stay in the hole they now live in or go to better quarters makes no difference."

It should be pondered by such opinionated people that society at large is often responsible for not having previously accepted, nutured, and prepared "those people" for living in their adopted communities in a better way.

The Inner City

In modern times, the study of urban conditions has always included awareness of poor areas, of areas of the prevalence of low economic conditions, of the *slums*. These have not always been the exact central districts in a city, geographically speaking. They are the areas anywhere in the city with the highest concentration of social problems.

Such areas are increasingly referred to as the "inner city." In these locations social disorganization is usually the greatest. There might be some psychological sense in which they are referred to as somehow different from the rest of the city. There might even be a bit of rejection of the troublesome area, almost a wish that it would vanish, because of the vexing problems which multiply within it.

The decaying sections of cities, or even the slightly worn older sections, are usually very complex areas. The ghetto, which is itself within the inner city, is by comparison a tightly homogeneous entity. In the inner city surrounding the ghetto and in addition to it there seem to be two other easily identifiable groupings within the heterogeneous mass of inner city dwellers. One is the run-down but still organized neighborhood, retaining some of the glories of its heyday, held together by its common associations like labor unions, political activities, churches, social clubs. The other is the rooming house district, noted for broken families, old-age pensioners, single individuals—whether previously used to close family ties or not, and physically and mentally less adequate people.

Some theoreticians differ with them, but many researchers contend and much experience confirms the following: The inner city is characterized by a high concentration of compounded social ills. Inner city social conditions are often identified with the term *blighted*. Blight is sometimes used as a designation for human decay and sometimes for property and other economic decay. The close correlations between these types of blight are not hard to see.

Sociologists Horton and Leslie give a condensed version of the factors composing blight. Their view may be true, but that it is true is due to society's dereliction to a large extent, in not having prevented or corrected at least a larger part of the evils:

Certain areas of the modern city may be likened to malignant growth on a living organism. They develop through the same processes that give life to the city as a whole, but they are largely parasitic, continuously growing, and they drain more and more of the city's lifeblood. These are blighted areas—the areas undergoing, or having undergone, deterioration. Crime, poverty, delinquency, prostitution, gambling, drug addiction, mental illness, tuberculosis, infant and maternal mortality, all are concentrated here. Rat-infested slums, filthy streets, crumbling buildings long since declared firetraps and frequently condemned, pawnshops, secondhand clothing stores, taverns, and "greasy spoons"—these are the physical habitat. Such blighted areas literally prey upon the rest of the city. The run-down buildings of the area pay relatively little in the way of taxes, though landlords often charge extremely high rents, and reap fantastic profits. The cost of providing police and fire protection, borne by the city at large, may be ten or twenty times as high as in other areas. The proportion of gainfully employed people is painfully low, and "relief" payments of all sorts flood into the area. Children play in the streets; there is no other place provided for them. Graduation from grade school is frequently followed by "matriculation" at reform school. Then it is an easy step to prison, all at the cost of $1200 or more each year which is furnished by the taxpayers. Health needs, if met at all, are handled by public health departments and by "free" clinics which are exorbitantly expensive for the public to maintain. Slum-clearance and low-cost housing is an additional form of subsidy. The modern slum embodies all that is un-American. The Promised Land?—a cruel joke! Faith in the future?—resignation and despair! Responsibility for self and family?—at the mercy of economic conditions and charitable agencies! A benefit of democracy?—ready-made propaganda for the totalitarian world! [9]

Lawrence K. Northwood categorizes the inner city under the headings of land use, population, and social control, in his study of inner city decay.[10] The one heartening aspect of so complex a field is that some parallel conditions are to be found in practically all large cities—heartening in the sense that perhaps further experience and research will guide urban specialists in more effective treatment of urban ills.

The Inner City and Race

It would be incorrect to say that there have not been race riots in America before the recent decade. Some of the worst ones during the Civil War and around the turn of the century were comparable to the Watts and Detroit riots of recent years. Race riots had to share the limelight with riots caused by religious antagonisms and ethnic friction. Whether or not it is because religious issues and even political issues do not raise as much emotion and cause as much conflict as was once the case, it is certainly true that the main area of intergroup friction is that of race. If more progress is not made in these relationships, insurrections like those of Nat Turner and John Brown will be repeated and exceeded.

Let us make no mistake. Race is a real factor in our society today, especially in our large cities. It is not possible to think of the large American cities apart from racial tensions in them.

It is proper to speak of the unity of the human race and to work toward a single society. It is no conflict with these concepts to acknowledge the reality of racial differences as accentuated by different skin colors. Emphasis *should* be on God's having created us all "of one blood" [11] but this truth does not erase the outward visible difference which still remains. Man still looks on the outward appearance and the Lord looks on the heart.[12]

The most intense social conflict of the day was spawned by man's greed and hate and has settled on the one characteristic of pigmentation. For being only skin deep, race is an explosive issue. It is proof, if ever the evangelical wanted any proof, of man's strange preoccupation with external factors as symbols and indicators of inner turmoil. What an opportunity the evangelical has today to tell his fellow men of the depravity of the human heart and of the power of God to make a man a new creature in Christ! [13]

References for Chapter 3
1. N.A.C.C.D., *Report*, p. 51.
2. *Ibid.*, p. 54.
3. *Ibid.*, p. 117.
4. *Ibid.*, p. 267; some other such conditions are described on pp. 48, 57, 59, 262, 267, 268.
5. Matthew 7:12.
6. N.A.C.C.D., *op. cit.*, p. 363.
7. *Ibid.*, p. 22.

8. *Ibid.*, p. 12, footnote 1.

9. Paul B. Horton and Gerald R. Leslie, *The Sociology of Social Problems* (New York, Appleton-Century-Crofts, 3rd ed., 1965), pp. 467, 469.

10. Lawrence K. Northwood, "Deterioration of the Inner City," in Nathan E. Cohen (ed.), *Social Work and Social Problems* (New York, National Association of Social Workers, 1964), pp. 206, 207.

11. Acts 17:26.

12. 1 Samuel 16:7.

13. 2 Corinthians 5:17.

4

Poverty

Poverty a Social Problem

Poverty is something we think of as a single problem. It is a problem, but is itself composed of many other social problems. It causes some problems and results from others.

Of all widespread social problems, poverty is the most ubiquitous. There is scarcely an area of any size inhabited by man where there is not some poverty.[1] On the American scene, poverty appears more concentrated in inner city and ghetto areas, and has been found to be on a large scale in rural areas as well. It sometimes takes in large sections of entire regions, as in Appalachia.

Poverty may be so severe and its victims so subject to its domination that there may be little or no resistance to it even within the hearts of the poverty-stricken. In most cases it causes a feeling of frustration and of resistance. Economic deprivation is added to all other aspects of poverty and combines with them to cause social unrest on however small or large a scale the circumstances may warrant.

In social action movements of our time other causes may be real enough, but without poverty as a contributing factor or even the major issue there would be little impetus to start social action movements on a large scale and of an extreme nature.

The Nature of Poverty

In one sense, poverty is a relative term. Mollie Orshansky discusses this fact, writes of its reality, and adds: "There is no reason to count the poor unless you are going to do something about them." [2]

Poverty may be relative and abstract as a philosophical or an economic term. Poor people are absolute and real, and suffer real suffering. Because poverty harms people, we dare to say that poverty, for purposes of our discussion, is absolute and real. As Roy Wilkins, executive director of the National Association for the Advancement of Colored Peoples, has said, "No American who is literate or reasonably attentive to passing events can be ignorant of the existence of millions of poor people of all races and colors in our affluent country." [3]

Poverty has caused widespread attention in our nation, but never before has it caused disruption on so wide a scale in our society. Kenneth Davis does not overstate it in referring to poverty as, "a phenomenon whose persistence is a personal tragedy for many Americans, an insult to the intelligence and morality of the community as a whole, and an increasingly grave threat to the survival of our free institutions." [4]

Definitions of Poverty

In laymen's terms, poverty might be termed as not having enough money to get along, or, living without having enough of the basic necessities of life.

Definitions of poverty arrived at the Office of Economic Opportunity and by the Social Security Administration are the usual type definitions used in governmental circles. "These definitions are usually food-oriented. That is, a certain minimum human diet was assigned current costs every year. It was then arbitrarily assumed that any household which had to spend more than one-third of its income to procure this minimum diet was poor. So a 'poverty threshold' was calculated for each different size of household by tripling the cost of providing the minimum diet for that number of persons. (A slightly different procedure was used for farm families . . .) Any household of a given size with an annual income less than this 'threshold' is considered poor." [5]

A study group of participants in a seminar for teachers of social welfare on an undergraduate level attempted a more inclusive definition, which takes into account many life factors:

Poverty exists when a person or persons are unable to participate in life adequately with sufficient benefit to themselves owing to one or more of the following:
  a. Lack of money
  b. Lack of good health
  c. Lack of marketable skills
  d. Lack of employment, under-employment, and lack of suitable employment
  e. Lack of education
  f. Lack of psychosocial acceptance and adequate social functioning. [6]

The Increase of Poverty Through the Years

The rapid growth of cities in America in the last two hundred years has been due to industrialization. The beginning of the factory system was marked by the need for labor to operate the new large machines located in the early factories. Movement of people to the cities to operate the machinery was one of the causes of a great increase in urban population.

A second development, immigration, took place as newcomers from foreign lands streamed into the United States in the last one hundred fifty years. They came especially in three great waves in the nineteenth and early twentieth centuries. A very large percentage of these immigrants clustered in the cities.

A third factor of major significance in urban population growth is the influx into the cities of America's agrarian population. Ninety percent rural and ten percent urban in population ratio in 1820, American population figures may show the exact opposite by the year 2000. As it is, the farm population within the nonurban total as of the year 1967 comprised six percent of the total population of the nation.

Poverty came with many of the new urbanites. It developed for others after they arrived. With the possible exception of early towns like Philadelphia and a few planned communities in more recent years, towns and cities have grown by accretion and have been molded very much as commercial and industrial interests have made them.

In the area of urban problems it should be noted that as the earlier settlers moved out and newer ones moved in, there was little if any city planning about how to accommodate immigrants and other newcomers. We as a nation have characteristically invited the oppressed to our shores, only to expect them in the last century and a quarter to live under urban conditions which are themselves oppressive. Marion O. Robinson writes, "Each group encountered the same experiences on the way up the ladder. As one professor of sociology ruefully puts it, 'segregated residence in slum areas, work with the lowest pay, hostility, prejudice, and discriminatory practices have never been reserved for any one newcomer or minority group. They have been democratically available to all newcomers without regard to race, religion, or origin. This has been the American Way.'" [7]

Many present intolerable living conditions of the poor are the result of many decades of deterioration. Whether or not much more is done in the fields of urban renewal, urban relocation, or model cities programs, something must be done to correct the conditions of shambles in our cities.

Many property owners have let their properties decay while they have indulged themselves in their own luxuries and built up their own financial and material interests.

Referring to others, property owners or not, who have left the inner city, we note that many such citizens have relinquished the opportunity and responsibility of governing and at the same time guiding the newcomers by moving away.

Consciously or unconsciously, *we* who are of wealth, or at least some degree of economic adequacy by comparison with the poor, feel that we are chosen of God to control material goods; that *they*—the urban poor—must somehow be unworthy because they are not economically well off. This, in spite of the fact that *we* have not in so many ways given *them* sufficient ways of achieving the same economic status as ourselves. We point to the comparatively few who carve out a place of eminence with us, and imply that others would be *up there* too if they weren't lazy. We insist on a *laissez faire* policy of expecting natural processes somehow to help the newcomers. We either keep our own guard up at the same time, to be sure not too many achieve the high goals we have reached, or we do not go out of our way to facilitate their improvement.

American blacks are again at hand to illustrate our point:

Negro migrations from the South have developed into major migrations to the inner cities, where black ghettos are formed. Especially in the older cities of the United States, they were expected to settle in areas already dilapidated after being worn out by successive groups of German, Irish, Italian, East European, Jewish, Spanish-American, and many other immigrants. The great majority of these had at least one common denominator—poverty. As they moved out, some of these several kinds of people from such diverse backgrounds also moved up economically. Many of them joined with earlier settlers in decrying the spread of nonwhite influence.

Only a few of the blacks who migrated knew much else than varying degrees of real poverty. The crime and shame of it is that they have been expected to stay in poverty.

It is bad enough that deliberate attempts have been and are being made to keep them in such conditions. By far the greater factor in poverty has been that the victims have been considered part of the subculture of poverty as part of the ascribed, almost assigned, status in life. The *Report* of the National Advisory Commission on Civil Disorders defines what it calls the "culture of poverty" and many writers on the subject discuss the "subculture of poverty." [8]

Rediscovery of Poverty

The degree to which poverty had been denied by our American society is shown by an incident which occurred in the late fifties, before poverty was brought back into national attention. A layman asked the writer why the rescue mission, of which the writer was then superintendent, was in existence. Was it not true that there were no poor any longer since the advent of public welfare on a large scale? Was it not true that when there were needs for help, the people could go to *the relief?* The same layman was chagrined to learn that there were many needs which could not be met by public welfare agencies, and that the authorities were only too glad to have private auspices like the mission to assist in such instances. He also learned to his surprise that there were so many emergencies and so few public welfare workers to cope with them that the welfare officials were glad to have mission assistance. This was in the form of supplementary relief, which the mission provided during the four to eight days at that time required to investigate the needs of the applicants and then to authorize and supply the funds needed.

Today, there is a different atmosphere. Instead of denying or being unaware of poverty, writers are outdoing one another in estimating poverty as affecting one-sixth or more of the population.

The present day is not the first period in our history in which poverty has been felt, recognized, and combated. Merton and Nisbet refer to the "continual rediscovery of the poor—an example of what Pitirim Sorokin called the Columbus complex. The poor, it seems, are perennially hidden, and the enterprising publicists of each decade reiterate their previous invisibility and regularly proclaim the distinctive and special qualities of the 'new poor.'" [9]

Today's rediscovery of the poor is a major event. It is of supreme importance in the question of national survival. Neglected, poverty could be a major agent of national disintegration. One figure suggested, that of thirty-six million poor, is a formidable figure. Of these, twenty-two million are in the cities and fourteen million in rural areas. One thing is certain: The poor are not likely soon again to allow themselves to be forgotten.

National recognition of poverty was given on a large scale during the Great Depression. Public assistance programs particularly served to meet subsistence needs of the people. Today, not only are public assistance payments usually inadequate, but large groups of the poor are not helped at all. Increased living costs and insufficient appropriations are partly to blame. Another factor is the limited nature of our Social Security programs by which some poor cannot get some benefits because they are not able to pay into the program.

In today's emergency, the Economic Opportunity Act with its resultant Office of Economic Opportunity has functioned to assist yet more of the needy. Both public assistance and Anti-Poverty programs have been literally lifesavers and enabling programs for many of the poor. Both programs have limitations and inadequacies, even abuses, of program, coverage and operation. Some people have taken unfair advantage of both and such people have lapsed into welfare dependency or welfare "chiseling" ways of life. Both programs have suffered from inadequate supply and training of workers.

Nevertheless, the government *is* doing something. It is not possible for private or church philanthropy to meet the needs of more than a small percentage of the needy without the government having to help others. Regardless of who is at fault for this fact, or how it got beyond nongovernment auspices to do very much about this, the fact remains that government is needed now in welfare. Even if it were thought desirable to remove government from welfare involvement, it would be impossible to do it without harm to the needy.

Government and Church Against Poverty

Governments have variously ignored or acknowledged poverty. Those that ignore it sometimes topple from power. As long ago as 430 B.C., Pericles said, "The real disgrace of poverty (is) not in owning to the fact but in declining the struggle against it." [10] Governments have had to be increasingly active in fighting poverty since the onset of the Industrial Age, and of urban decay, which has been on the upgrade in the last one hundred fifty years and more.

President Herbert Hoover expressed belief that poverty in our nation could be greatly diminished, even banished: "We in America today are nearer to the final triumph over poverty than ever before in the history of any land. The poorhouse is vanishing from us. We have not yet reached the goal, but, given a chance . . . we shall soon with the help of God be in sight of the day when poverty will be banished from this nation." [11]

President Lyndon B. Johnson, as a concerned chief executive, acted in many ways to lead the nation in the correction of social distresses, particularly in launching the Anti-Poverty Program. He said, "A great nation is able to make and is willing to make a commitment to eradicate poverty among its people." [12]

It should be self-evident that the Church should be willing to work with the government in correction and prevention of major social problems. This is obligatory when it is within the Church's power to do so.[13]

The Church can help most by *understanding* public welfare and its methods and agencies.[14] Particularly is this important to understand at this crucial period of transition and projected change in welfare policy and operations. President Nixon's monumental welfare reform programs will bring to the fore questions both new and old. Who is eligible for welfare help? How shall welfare payments be made? How can help be delivered to those who need it most? How much money can be provided to underwrite welfare programs? Shall there be a guaranteed annual income? Negative income tax? And more.

On the individual level, it should be clear to each Christian that he should know enough about welfare services to know what types of assistance people on welfare are getting and even how they feel about welfare programs. How can a Christian deal with much effectiveness on a spiritual level with someone whose life is greatly affected by welfare services when the well-meaning Christian has not taken the trouble to find out more about his circumstances?

On a grander scale, government and Church alike must separately and together understand and cope with the poverty issue as political and religious bodies have never before done. Never before has it been possible to ascertain by research the nature and extent of poverty to the degree to which it is being done today. Peter L. Berger writes succinctly of the key issue: "The higher classes in our society are better fed, better housed, better educated, and live longer than their less fortunate fellow citizens. These observations may be truisms, but they gain in impact if one sees that there is a statistical correlation between the quantity of money one earns '*per annum*' and the number of years one may expect to do so on this earth." [15]

Christian Concern About Poverty

Certainly Christians want to do what they can to fight poverty.[16]

First, we need to realize that poverty will never be eliminated by human action. It can be dealt with successfully and controlled, reduced, or prevented to a large degree, as a social problem.

Second, poverty as a personal condition and attribute will always be with us as must be the case as long as there are richer and poorer people in the world. Jesus Himself while here during His first advent indicated that we always will have the poor with us.[17] (It is improper exegesis of this passage of Scripture to make it say that poor people must *remain* poor or that poverty is recommended as a condition in which to remain.)

References for Chapter 4

1. For one of many summaries of distribution of poverty in America, see Herman P. Miller's "Profile of the Poor," in his article, "Dimensions of Poverty," in Ben B. Seligman (ed.), *Poverty as a Public Issue* (New York, The Free Press paperback, 1965), pp. 28–30.
2. Mollie Orshansky, "How Poverty Is Measured," in "Perspectives on Poverty," Reprint No. 2604, Bureau of Labor Statistics, in *Monthly Labor Review* (February, 1969), p. 37.
3. Roy Wilkins, Editorial, "Critics of Poor Are Out of Step," *Philadelphia Evening Bulletin* (May 29, 1968), p. 15.
4. Kenneth S. Davis (ed.), *The Paradox of Poverty in America* (New York, the H. W. Wilson Co., 1969), p. 6.
5. Anthony Downs, "Who Are the Urban Poor?" *CED Supplementary Paper,* No. 26, October, 1968 (New York, Committee for Economic Development, 1968), p. 7.

6. Group 4, Charles Y. Furness, recorder, "Teaching Outline on Poverty," Council on Social Work Education, institute for social scientists teaching social welfare subjects, at Worden School of Social Service (San Antonio, Texas, July 14–20, 1969), *typed,* Group 4, Session 2, p. 2.

7. Marion O. Robinson, "Humanizing the City," *Public Affairs Pamphlet 417* (New York, Public Affairs Committee, 1968), p. 7.

8. N.A.C.C.D., *Report,* pp. 262, 263; also see Elizabeth Herzog, *About the Poor,* Children's Bureau Publication no. 451–1967 (Washington, D.C., U.S. Government Printing Office, 1967).

9. Robert K. Merton and Robert A. Nisbet, *Contemporary Social Problems* (New York, Harcourt, Brace and World, 2nd ed., 1966), p. 637.

10. Pericles' "Oration on the occasion of the funeral for Greeks slain in the Peloponnesian War," in Houston Peterson (ed.), *A Treasury of the World's Great Speeches* (New York, Simon and Schuster, 1954), p. 12.

11. Herbert C. Hoover, speech, November 8, 1928, quoted in Robert L. Heilbroner, *The Making of Economic Society* (Englewood Cliffs, N.J., 1st ed., 1962), p. 141.

12. Lyndon B. Johnson, statement on signing "The Economic Opportunity Act," Health, Education and Welfare *Indicators* (September, 1964), p. vi.

13. James 4:17; Proverbs 3:27, 28.

14. As used here, "public welfare" means all welfare programs paid for by the tax monies from and administered by all levels of government, local, county, state, federal. "Public assistance" is so often referred to as "welfare" or "relief" or "public welfare" but is only one part of public welfare provisions.

15. Berger, *Invitation to Sociology,* p. 80.

16. Wirt, *Social Conscience,* p. 136.

17. Matthew 26:11; Mark 14:7.

5

The *Big Four*

Vital Perspective

As these words are being written, quite a considerable time after the Newark riot of July, 1967, it is evident no major changes have taken place in race relations, basically. Outwardly there have been the gains of analysis of the causes of turbulence and some attempts to correct the problems. There have been some slight gains in employment of the poor (even in increasing general unemployment), as well as in some health provisions and some better education.

But attitudes? Polarizations, confrontations, for better or for worse.

As we mentioned earlier, mass media of communication can be expected to help assess problems and needs and help move toward solutions. Among other things, since the Kerner *Report,* we've had helpful documentaries on poverty, health, hunger, education of the blacks, and more.

So far, so good, as the saying goes; but, just as violence flared even after court victories, revealing even more elementary pressures and frustrations than could be cured by good but belated legislation, so might anger erupt if the basic needs of our poor millions are not met by more than has appeared on the horizon. Much hinges on pending welfare reforms, as we have said.

The Fourfold Backbone of Poverty

Of all the multiple causes of social unrest in our country today the most critical by far is the complex of factors by which the poor of our time are disadvantaged. Although many factors combine to create the juggernaut of poverty, nearly all discussions of poverty which are current today identify unemployment, poor education, poor housing, and poor health as the staples of which poverty is composed. These are like the bones which hold poverty upright.[1] These are the *big four*.

Each of the *big four* is a social problem in its own right. Together they make up a terrifying array which causes trouble both for those who are their victims and for other citizens against whom they incite their victims to act. In the wake of the Detroit and Newark riots of 1967, Sargent Shriver, then Director of the Office of Economic Opportunity, said:

The only genuine, the only permanent answer to preventing riots is to attack the causes which produce riots. First of all, when we overcrowd people into specialized areas or specific areas of a city, we're in trouble. When we don't have jobs for these people or job training for them, we're in trouble. When they've got poor housing, when they've got overcrowded schools . . . when there's nobody from the so-called "establishment" talking to them, listening to them, actually doing things with them—not for them, but *with them*—then we're in trouble. I don't know of a case so far where a riot occurred where these conditions which produce riots didn't exist before the riot . . . Everybody has got to make an exceptional and additional effort to meet the legitimate demands for jobs, for schooling, for health, for justice, for housing, for education, that the poor people of the United States are demanding and, in some cases, they are resorting to violence to show how desperately they want these opportunities, opportunities which truthfully all the rest of us Americans have enjoyed for a long time.[2]

The prominence of the *big four* in the above quotation is inescapable. The four meet the eye at every turn where riot causes are discussed in the *Report* of the National Advisory Commission on Civil Disorders.[3] These are the four which make up some of the flames of the antagonisms of our times. These antagonisms are fanned by the winds of discrimination and fed by the fuel of racisms. They are inadequately curbed by all the however well-meaning safeguards of legal enablement and public welfare programs. We see now that attempts must be made to contain and quench these flames by proper facing of the issues.

Unemployment

Far more than any one factor, unemployment has brought about the violence of recent years. Underemployment and unsuitable employment are associated irritants. Prolonged unemployment is a threat to human survival, or at least to living as long as a person might under happier and more adequate conditions. It militates against a level of living which includes decency and at least minimum adequacy of food and other necessities.

Some idea of the emergency in Negro unemployment may be seen in that there is frequent incidence of over six percent among blacks.[4] In some instances unemployment is up to twenty-five percent and more in some ghetto situations. As a point of comparison, it should be noted that three percent was a usual figure nationwide in 1967. It is approaching five percent and more in mid-1970.

Unemployment and poor employment situations are punitive. They militate against a person's beginning to arrive at or retaining a conscious sense of occupying a satisfactory status position in life. They keep him from feeling an equal sense of human dignity when with his fellows, when unemployment drags on and on through no fault of the unemployed person. "As Daniel P. Moynihan has written: 'The principal measure of progress toward equality will be that of employment. It is the primary source of individual or group identity. In America what you do is what you are: to do nothing is to be nothing; to do little is to be little. The equations are implacable and blunt, and ruthlessly public. For the Negro American it is already, and will continue to be the master problem.'" [5]

Why is it that only *now* the blacks have struck out against the larger structure? Is it that such a large amount of unemployment and job discrimination has only recently accumulated so that it is intolerable to remain subdued? Is it that Negroes have had a taste of what they formerly thought inaccessible and now they want it?

Automation

Although progress is not as fast as it should have been in the economic betterment of American blacks, there was until recently the idea among some of them that advance would eventually accelerate, or at least hope was entertained to that end.

Then came automation.

Immediate and long range views of economic and labor developments envision a society of greater production and consumption and more leisure. Admittedly, now, regardless of the future, automation means *elimination* of jobs by the thousands. These are the jobs that are held by unskilled and semiskilled workers. These are the very jobs held by the poor, including blacks. They usually have no way of training for other jobs, even if they have inclination for it. There is the grave question as to what jobs, if any, could be gotten instead of the ones from which they have been displaced.

Writers on automation point out the *temporary* dislocations caused by automation. Parallels are drawn to the way the industrial revolutions of the past two hundred years caused temporary dislocations and great hardship to those who lost jobs as machinery displaced people. It is concluded by those drawing the parallels that growth and change inevitably cause hardships during the transition period. Nevertheless, it is no easier today than it was then for any individual to be permanently cut off from his livelihood, no matter how temporary are the inconveniences suffered by the changing society at large. Indeed, it is harder for most urban dwellers who are discarded than for many in former days who had more family and friendship connections in rural areas to fall back on.

As Walter Buckingham points out, the prime focus is not on unemployment of those who could work at given jobs when they can get work, but on displacement of the unemployed who become unable to return to their job because there is no longer *their job* available anywhere.[6] If one adds to this the unavailable or unlikely retraining for other jobs and the age and health of the displaced worker, some of the grimness of this kind of social change becomes evident.

The crux of the matter is that in a money economy there are hazards to individuals who cannot enter the labor market as their counterparts formerly could do, because of the nonexistence of jobs they previously held, or who cannot make enough money at what is available in their line. Some hardship is caused as better jobs are eliminated and those who formerly held them are expected to work in jobs below their ability or in jobs of low status. The four Ss—survival, status position, satisfaction, and self-fulfillment—are best realized, it is being said in many quarters today, through provision of an adequate standard of living considered as the right of the individual.[7]

It is not at this point vital to enter into current debate about work as contrasted with or combined with guaranteed minimum income where no work is available, or negative income tax combined with work. The important factor to note regardless of the means to its achievement is the pressing need to provide the poor with the minimum essentials of life. This providing for the poor, in keeping with the best biblical and social welfare standards, includes expecting the ones needing the help to earn it by working when possible. Where this is not possible, as in so many cases it is not, the needs must be met otherwise.

A concerned layman may recommend or oppose one device or another for providing minimum income. Using or not using a plan or theory will not eliminate responsibility for facing in all possible ways this most crucial of all the justifiable complaints of the disadvantaged man, that he does not have the minimum essentials of life.

While most blacks will not express it in words, they are very aware of the truth enunciated by Oscar Handlin: "The rate of economic and social change in the United States is so rapid that a handicapped group feels ever further behind if it progresses more slowly than the rest of the population."

Automation is here to stay. How its ill effects are to be neutralized and its good effects favorably made use of, by and for the poor as well as others, is not entirely clear—but seeing how this is to be resolved is a *must* on the priority list of today's America.[9]

Education

It is currently evident that overcrowding is a major problem in ghetto and inner city schools. It is undeniable that educational facilities, curricula and quality of instruction are inferior also. One manifest reason for *white flight* from the cities is the desire of white parents to get better educational facilities for their children. With recent passage of open housing legislation, it will be at least theoretically possible for blacks also to go out of the inner city with more facility than before to seek better education.

It is hard to visualize poor educational conditions without actually seeing and working with parents, educators, and children in the inner cities. Exposure to gangs, delinquency, vice, crime, gambling, and the use of narcotics including alcohol are poorly combatted by ghetto schools. For too many pupils, these schools are little more than places to pass their time if indeed they attend at all. Poor education is greatly prejudicial in job procurement and job performance. Blacks, poor or otherwise, are more disadvantaged than whites the less education they have. Even when blacks are well educated they are all too often not given equal job opportunities with white workers.[10]

Housing

Further insight into poor housing and poor health in poverty areas is best gained by looking at a few instances of the prevailing conditions. One such scene is described as follows: "in vast areas of dilapidated housing where living conditions . . . were so bad that 'people would be kinder to their pets,' were Negro migrants, Cubans and Puerto Ricans." [11]

Showing the relationship of intolerable living conditions to domestic problems, the National Advisory Commission on Civil Disorders *Report* says: "Living on marginal incomes in cramped and deteriorating quarters—one-third of the housing was overcrowded and more than half sub-standard—families were breaking up at an increasing rate." [12]

It is certain that no real social improvement is likely unless improvement programs for meeting the personal and familial needs of the people are made paramount. It is fashionable to find fault with public welfare and public housing programs, and not without cause. New programs are often inadequate before their actual construction or realization takes place, as is being said of the model cities programs. It is currently promised that social needs of the people will be given priority in planning and not fixtures and furnishings instead. Time will tell.

Health

Inadequate nourishment and malnutrition are almost universal among America's poor, whether rural or urban, white or black, or otherwise. The relationship of this fact to behavior is not hard to see.

Wayne Yaeger, District Public Health Director in Valdosta, Georgia, speaks about "borderline starvation" in a newspaper article: " 'You are correct in stating that many Americans suffer from an improper diet and it is a problem of education and personal decisions.' Yaeger wrote '. . . The trouble is that it is most difficult to educate a poorly motivated, half-starved under-nourished citizen.' He said, 'It is also not practical to expect good, sound decision-making in individuals who are getting by nutritionally on enriched starches and low-protein intake.' " [13]

Looking from the local health district to the national scene, we note that efforts of the government to correct poor health needs, especially in the area of food for survival and better nutrition, reflect the seriousness of health crises. Efforts of the Senate investigating committee chaired by Senator George McGovern and recent pronouncements on health needs by President Richard M. Nixon should help dispel attempts to belittle the seriousness of this crisis.

Many sources support the contention that the poor are less healthy and live shorter lives than others.[14] They have more mental illness, suffer more frequently from major diseases, and have greater susceptibility to infection.

It is poignantly clear to anyone working constantly with people in need that some groups of people appear more beset with misery than others. In the field of physical misery, the three largest such subgroups of poor and chronically-ill people are the alcoholics, the senile, and the mentally ill of the long-term variety. There may soon be a comparable group of drug addicts.

A Word About Causation

The evangelical Christian should guard against oversimplification when he talks about causes of violence. It is easy to say that sin is at the root of riots and other disorders. It *is* certain that sin *is* at the root. The question is, *Whose* sin? Who is more at fault, the one who lashes out against indescribable living conditions or the one who is not even aware that his American fellow citizen is suffering so extremely while he does nothing to help?

Violent action will persist until legitimate grievances of the poor are realized and sincere efforts are made to cope with the problems causing them, on a more adequate scale than is now the case. Violent action stemming from less fundamental causes will be hard to stir up if basic needs of the poor are met, especially needs for employment, education, housing and health.

Alvin E. Echols, Jr., Executive Director of the North City Congress, Philadelphia, writes in this vein also:

The Black Community needs the same social and economic options which the white community has always had—that is all. Black people need living wages and meaningful labor—or a guaranteed annual income. They need openings to reside where they wish to earn and enjoy that income—both inside and outside the ghetto. And black children need education of a quality sufficient to prepare and project them into all walks of life. Until the Black Community has all these options, it will not and cannot relax. When white tension gets translated into a commitment to social change, black tension will decline. Until then, we are bound to have irritation, strain, disruption, violence—all the hallmarks of progress trying to come about in short order.[15]

References for Chapter 5

1. See Leonard J. Duhl, "Planning and Poverty," in Leonard J. Duhl (ed.), *The Urban Condition* (New York, Basic Books, 1963), p. 296.
2. Sargent Shriver, in *War on Poverty*, O.E.O. News Summary, Vol. 11–19, July 24, 1967 (Washington, D.C., U.S. Government Printing Office), p. 1.
3. N.A.C.C.D., *Report*, pp. 82, 83.
4. *Ibid.*, pp. 10, 13.
5. *Ibid.*, p. 252.
6. Walter Buckingham, *Automation*, in Leonard Freedman and Cornelius P. Cotter (eds.), *Issues of the Sixties* (Belmont, Calif., Wadsworth Publishing Co., 1961), pp. 224–232.
7. National Association of Social Workers, *Goals of Public Social Policy* (New York, National Association of Social Workers, 1967), pamphlet, pp. 53–55.
8. Oscar Handlin, *Fire-Bell in the Night* (Boston, Little, Brown and Co., 1964), p. 5.
9. N.A.C.C.D., *op. cit.*, pp. 13, 14.
10. *Ibid.*, pp. 50, 93.
11. *Ibid.*, p. 57.
12. *Ibid.*, p. 53.
13. Michael J. Posner, *Philadelphia Inquirer* (June 17, 1968), p. 5.
14. See American Journal of Nursing, "The Sick Poor," *American Journal of Nursing*, Vol. 69, No. 11 (November, 1969), 2423–2454.
15. Alvin E. Echols, Jr., Remarks, "Tensions—A Reality in the Black Community and in Philadelphia" (January 5, 1968), *mimeographed*, p. 5.

6

Communication

Closing the Communications Gap

Much has been made in recent years of the *communications gap* in human relationships.

The bare fact is that people in the United States of America, poverty-stricken as well as others, own or have access to radio and television. They know what world events are taking place. They are bombarded by commentators in print and by sound. They are sought and contacted by political, labor, and commercial interests with causes to plead or articles to sell.

There can no longer be a communications gap to the extent that there has previously been. The poor are no longer content to submit passively to decision-making by others on their behalf in matters in which they can and should participate in the decision-making process. This is all the more so now that they can be informed of issues and of ways of getting assistance in time of need. One epic of our day is tracing how the poor moved from a position of having to accept whatever anyone condescended to give them to a position of having enough bargaining power to make themselves heard on crucial issues of survival and progress.

The whole question of who will influence the poor in the days ahead is manifestly of great importance. Let us be clear about this: Evangelicals must minister to the poor and influence them for righteousness. To minister meaningfully we must receive communication *from* those to whom we minister in order best to communicate *with* them and *to* them—that is, frankly, we must receive communication from them in the form of learning about them and their needs in depth, and we must continue hearing what they say each day.

The Commission on Civil Disorders says: "City governments need new and more vital channels of communication to the residents of the ghetto; they need to improve their capacity to respond effectively to community needs before they become community grievances . . . ." [1]

Communication is more than transmission of information; it is making others partakers of our ideas. It is even harder to let others' ideas become ours. We are slow to receive people too different from ourselves, because of lack of knowledge of others, or unwillingness to accept them even if we do know them. We tend to see what is faulty about other people. Others often see only what is faulty about us.

White Conceptions of the Blacks

Again the American Negroes illustrate a point, this time as the misunderstood people in illustrating how some people fail to understand others who are different from themselves.

How the blacks have been viewed in the past in America is still strongly influencing how they are viewed in the present. It is only some forty years since some standard descriptions of Negroes have been revised to describe them as humans equal with others, instead of inferior to them. When they were slaves they were considered human beings, but as inferior humans in the eyes of their masters and many other people. As a labor commodity in the economy of our republic's early years, they were classified and treated as property by many. Originally, even the United States Constitution counted a Negro as only three-fifths of a person. That was specified, until later amended, in Article I, Section 2, Clause 3, and was stipulated for the purpose of counting population for purposes of representation and taxation. This was changed by Amendments XIII in 1865, XIV in 1868, and XV in 1870. In the course of these Amendments the Negroes were guaranteed freedom, civil rights, and political rights they had not possessed before. The key sections in counting each Negro as one person instead of three-fifths are Section 2 of Amendment XIV, and Section 1 of Amendment XV.

It is not generally known by many that a considerable number of slave owners considered the Negro as an animal, and some considered him to have no soul.[2]

Social Darwinism and other evolutionary ideas did not help any, because white scholars in some instances were evidently swayed by current notions of Negro inferiority and relegated them to inferior places in their categories of human development. This did not change considerably until early in this century and is still in process of change.

Whether such low views of the blacks were purposely thus held or not is not the point. The fact is that they *were* held, sincerely or not. Some of the slaveholders did not want their own world to fall. Others who were afraid of the economic consequences to them if the slaves were freed, or otherwise educated and trained attempted to keep them in ignorance. Such men were known to assert that blacks should be kept in ignorance. This was one factor which worked to deny most blacks any formal education on a large scale until quite recently. Slave owners reasoned that slaves would be handicapped with no education and would be better kept in ignorance and thus better prevented from rising up against their masters. J. Oliver Buswell,

III, quotes one writer as saying, "The slaveholders . . . had either to let the institution gradually pass away or close all avenues of information to the minds of their Negroes." [3]

Education is a form of communication. The education of the Negro is a most vital concern for us now. In the light of extremely hostile attitudes of some white people, past and present, is it any wonder that blacks were and are kept in ignorance and kept in lower level jobs?

Mutual Responsibility and Collaboration

It should be understood that both white and black alike should feel responsible when either shows animosity for the other. Racism is a form of ethnocentrism and is evidenced in exalting one's group above any other and insisting on separation of it from others, if that separation is to proclaim superiority over and opposition to other groups. White racists have long evidenced hatred for Negroes, Jews, foreigners. It is also not a new thing for blacks to show exclusiveness from outsiders in an antagonistic way, as is showing up in some extremist black power groups today.

White power and black power movements today range from extreme to moderate, from constructive to destructive. What is needed is for whites and blacks alike to collaborate in helping to solve the problems of the poor.

Black capitalism is one move in the direction of developing black potential and helping blacks in the process. The operation of black business ventures mainly for blacks is a constructive outgrowth of ghetto crises. The development of Opportunities Industrialization Centers founded by Rev. Leon Sullivan is a black self-help movement indigenous to the black subculture. What is also good about both the black capitalism and the self-help programs is that they attempt to help all in need, black or not, even though most of their work is focused necessarily on the black community.

White-based groups like the Urban Coalition and the National Alliance of Businessmen are at least trying to set programs in motion which might eventually make great contributions to the needs of the unemployed. However, they have such factors to contend with as providing jobs that are really necessary rather than *make-work* and are performed for adequate pay; understanding cultural and educational differences of the poor and especially those who may be racially or ethnically different; and convincing whites that blacks are basically equal with them and ought to be given equal opportunity as they work alongside the whites.

Black Power

One solution to pressing needs among the poor is certainly the use of black power. The use of black manpower and other assets of the blacks to solve their own problems and stand with other Americans against common problems can be applauded by whites. Black power of the violent kind is not even the same kind of thing.

Of the wise use of black power, Echols says, "How does the black community achieve the strength to bring about change? The Black Power movement is a home-grown answer . . . a 'solution' which the black community has built for itself and which . . . grows enormously fast toward maturity as the expressive social movement of that community." [4]

Facing Rejection by the Rejected

Once the evangelical Christian understands the forces by which the blacks were kept segregated for so long a time and

the reality of both white and black racisms in further polarizations today, he must face the reality of rejection by blacks.

The evangelical is rejected because he has not taken the
evangel to the blacks nor much other help and love that he
should have delivered. He may be rejected because he is white,
or, in the instance of the black evangelical, because he is so
closely identified with the white man's gospel. Of somewhat
different category is the black evangelical who has little or no
connection with whites and is accepted fully by the blacks without hindrance of white stigma.

At the same time that the white evangelical must be prepared
to face rejection, he should not forget that there are some white
and black evangelicals who have always worked together and
have ministered to blacks. He must patiently admit that neglect
has occurred, even if not in every case. The Christian worker
might be faced with attitudes seen in words like those written
by a black recipient of help after this writer had directed the
resources of the Goodwill Home and Rescue Mission, Newark,
New Jersey, to provide help (in 1963):

"I fully appreciate your every effort by helping my wife and
me, also trying to win us to Christ. But one thing I must mention,
not to make you mad but only to impress upon your mind one
thing: Why are Negroes claimed by the white man to be an
outcast or in so many words rejected—because their skins are
dark. They are looked upon as animals. You want us to accept
your way of teaching . . . but yet you won't accept us on equal
terms as you do your own. When the white man begins to look
at us Negroes as human beings, as they do any or most other
races, . . . then maybe we will be convinced that your ideas,
and ideals of God are O.K., when you'll accept us Negroes as
you do your own. I want to accept God on my own terms when
I am ready."

Evident in the above quotation are several issues of racial animosity and inequality we have been discussing. Some who read this might seize upon the last sentence quoted, to dismiss all that went before it as only an excuse to evade God's claims. There is indeed an element of this, but there is another factor fully evident. Because Christians have not presented God and the gospel effectively, the blacks in America often have difficulty seeing God.

As we realize that the Church as a whole has evidently let the Negro stay to himself in religious matters, we must remember that some evangelization of the blacks was done in earlier times in our nation and its predecessor colonies. Because of this, true Christian faith has often been the stay of godly Negroes in time of trouble as well as of joy. There were also some godly slave owners who ministered the gospel to their slaves and lived a life of love and kindness to them. After the blacks were freed, they lost no time in organizing their own denominational churches. What is needed next is for white and black evangelicals to show their solidarity of faith and witness.

Some Backgrounds of White Exclusiveness

Some deliberate withholding of the gospel from blacks is a matter of record. As Albert Barnes, writing in 1846, said: "'I have never seen one (of the gentlemen of the slaveholding states) who would not admit that the gospel would ultimately remove slavery entirely.'" [5]

Accordingly, there was deliberate neglect of the duty to communicate the gospel to the blacks on the part of many who were not constrained by the love of Christ to get the gospel to their own slaves. In the case of freed slaves, the responsibility devolved upon Christians elsewhere in the country to evangelize them, and many of these failed to communicate the gospel to them.

Another view of the reasons for the white minimum of inter-action with minority groups stems from alleged differences in philosophies of colonization. According to this opinion, Spanish and French settlers colonized to search for gold and new trade routes. On the other hand, the English are said to have con-centrated upon setting up their own distinct colonial units for permanence. Because of religious and political pressures formerly brought to bear upon them, including persecution, they became accustomed to keeping separate from outsiders. As much as they could and without mingling very much with the Indians or set-tlers from other nations, they kept themselves racially or reli-giously *pure*. They tended to make each immigrant minority group win their way into acceptance by measuring up to their social and economic requirements. In most instances the im-migrant minorities were white. How accurate this opinion is poses a question, but it seems plausible to a good degree.

It was different in the case of the blacks. The racial barrier was the most unacceptable factor. In addition, the blacks have for so very long a time not had capital or job opportunities equal to those of the whites, and have suffered discrimination as se-verely as and very often more severely than the other minority groups that preceded them.

The Blacks Come Into Their Own

We have already spoken of the recent Supreme Court decisions like those of 1954 and 1964 on matters of education and voting rights. It is too bad that such decisions are necessary these days, when it is easy to see that these rights are in the Bill of Rights of the Constitution as well as in Amendments XIII, XIV, and XV. Nevertheless, as long as it has taken most nonblacks a hundred years to catch up with the intent of the law, it is good to have these reminders.

While we realize that the black Americans are completely part of us, and bring our minds along with our hearts to accept them, why not try to win their acceptance of us, instead of always feeling that they have to win our acceptance? If we wait for them to want to win ours, we will have a long wait if we do not want to win theirs.

References for Chapter 6

1. N.A.C.C.D., *Report*, p. 16.
2. Ariel (pen-name for B. H. Payne), *The Negro: What Is His Ethnological Status?* 1867, quoted in James O. Buswell, *III, Slavery, Segregation and Scripture* (Grand Rapids, Mich., Wm. B. Eerdmans, 1954), pp. 23, 24.
3. C. G. Woodson, *The Education of the Negro Prior to 1861* (1915), quoted in Buswell, *op. cit.*, pp. 34, 35.
4. Echols, *Tensions*, p. 3.
5. Albert Barnes, *An Inquiry Into the Scriptural Views of Slavery* (1846), p. 366, quoted in Buswell, *op. cit.*, p. 34.

7

Conflict

Understanding Social Action in Historical Perspective

Thirty or forty years ago, many Christians disliked the terms social justice and social action because they were associated with socialistic and communistic activities. While this antipathy is still somewhat the case, our dislike of the term social action today is largely because much that is violent is called by that name.

Not all social action is violent or unpleasant, by any means. Whether pleasant or unpleasant, it is necessary to study social action, and to understand the action and the people involved in it. The people make the effort worthwhile. For the sake of helping people, Christians ought to apply themselves to understanding violent social action so as to know what should replace it.

One pleasant aspect of social action is experienced when people of like mind although of two different *kinds* act unitedly because they are working toward social and economic improvements. Negro leader Charles Evers is quoted as saying, "I will continue to fight to make Mississippi a better place for both black and white . . . We've got to live together and work together as human beings." [1]

One important goal Americans should have is to use knowledge of historical perspective to help avoid conflicts like those of the past. Instead, we often focus on the long past of conflict to place and perpetuate blame for injustices. This is all right if people of the present are repeating the injustices perpetrated by their predecessors. What is desirable is objective and levelheaded evaluation of the present problems to identify and place only as much blame as should be on any side of a question. Then correction should take place followed by adoption of better procedures for the future. "It is less important to ascribe the blame for past errors than to locate the responsibility for future decisions." [2]

It is still true that most blacks want to be fully recognized as Americans and only a few, however vocal, oppose considering America as their homeland. Will we improve living conditions for blacks and other minority group members so they will continue to view our nation as their home instead of as their prison? Will we understand their own attempts to help themselves when they can, and their protests when they cannot?

Economic pressures have forced protest by the poor of our nation. Will we hear this cry for help, or will twentieth-century Christians repeat the honest but costly mistake of some religious leaders in the past when they urged the nobles to suppress the peasantry who had cried out against major economic and social abuses? Perhaps a small minority were extremists, personally obnoxious, and politically unpalatable; nevertheless, thousands upon thousands of peasants had many major unmet needs.

Understanding Violence

The fact of the slowness of change normally and the fact of emergency pressures upon the poor have been recently dramatized again in the 1968 Poor People's Campaign. Attorney General Clark properly insisted that "we have got to move within the framework of the law . . . ." [3]

Socioeconomic pressures have sparked sit-ins, marches, and

demonstrations. Has the climax of the present series of legal advances on behalf of the poor been reached, and have accompanying demonstrations reached their finish?

It is not good to be lulled to sleep in the face of continuing strife, even though that strife may be in a calmer stage at present. There is some belief that there is no significant movement to improve conditions reported by the Commission on Civil Disorders, and even some worsening of them. Commentator Simeon Booker currently keeps his public posted on how he sees Nixon administration attitudes toward the blacks, sometimes favorable to them, sometimes the opposite. The late Dr. Ralph Bunche was reported (mid-1970) as saying that new protests by Negroes could be expected if their needs were not attended to.

The first step in preparing for protests is to do that very thing, attend to legitimate needs. The second is to ascertain whether any possible disorders are predictable in the near future. Are they likely to be led by truly concerned leaders who feel their people cannot wait for redress of wrongs [4] by slower legislative and fiscal change, or by the type of militants motivated mostly by antagonism?

It is fairly evident that no master plan of subversion brought about the riots of 1967. It appeared that each of the towns and cities affected had its own set of local circumstances and personalities reacting to the stimuli peculiar to its own situations.

It is accordingly necessary to look behind the disruptive methods to see the people and the common needs they had, even though disturbances took place in widely separated parts of the country. As this was done, and the *big four* plus racism and discrimination emerged in view, a pattern was set that ought to be duplicated: Careful investigation of reasons and causes. Something largely lacking from the 1967 riots should take place in the event of future disturbances: a master plan of meeting needs, or at least an honest attempt to meet them by all involved. It goes without saying that preventive measures are always in order where possible.

Also indicated: If the disruption that might take place is because wronged people believe that they have no other recourse than to take *direct action,* their complaints should be dealt with on their merits or lack of them and they should not be summarily turned away when they have legitimate grievances. If the disruption is spearheaded by agitators, the agitators should be dealt with, as such, while legitimate needs of the people they lead are considered fairly.

An urgent reason Christians should know about violence in the context of today's social action movements is that violence is being espoused by some religious leaders. They are influenced by the trends of the times into thinking it an act of championing the downtrodden to *identify* with them in using violence.

Some such religious leaders believe such action to be a part of their ministry. Others quite likely engage in these tactics as a substitute for a ministry that does not otherwise satisfy them in usual pastoral duties, whatever the reasons may be that it does not.

The Christian and Violence

What of the evangelical Christian? Is there nothing he can do to improve the lot of the poor without resort to violence?

The individual Christian should note the fact reflected in the following editorial: "until the two-thirds of the American people who belong to churches assume a personal obligation in regard to national problems, the Christian community will not be guiltless for the rising tide of violence. Nor will it be showing itself a viable force within this country, much less the salt of the earth." [5]

Does this mean that evangelical Christian church members within the *two-thirds* must go along with whatever other nominal Christians do? Manifestly not! It is a travesty upon Christianity— even if in the guise of helping the poor—to advocate and partici- pate in direct violence.

We do not say that Christians cannot do *any* outward pro- testing against injustices, providing the injustices are truly that and providing protest methods are within the law. This we shall consider more fully, but even more important now is to remember that the evangelical has a very important status to remember:

The Christian is a representative of the Prince of Peace. He is enjoined by the Scriptures to pursue peace.[6] As he does so, he acts in character when he occasionally initiates some helpful action.

Four things a Christian may do, at least: He may seek a change in laws and associated procedures in helping those who are in need; he may work through community channels to help meet human need; he may work through his own church ministries to facilitate their effectiveness among those in need; and he may perform any of several services as an individual, as the Lord gives him opportunity.

Demonstrations

As Dr. George Davis says, "Demonstrations held the potential of something far different than what they started out to be."[7]

Some concerned evangelicals felt, when such demonstrations as the March to Montgomery took place, that this was a way for evangelical Christians to register support for the right of minority groups to exercise their constitutional rights. This was seen as a defense of the right to demonstrate in cases of "abridgement of the right to vote and peaceable assembly to petition the government for redress of grievances." [8]

It could not be foreseen by these same evangelicals that in so short a time many of those they joined in demonstrating would be advocating in ecumenical councils that there should be use of "open violence as a legitimate means by which the Church can help to transform society." [9]

Such violence was advocated in Detroit, at the United States Conference on Church and Society, sponsored by the National Council of Churches, October 22–26, 1967. This amounted to "irony" in that, "At a time when the Church's resources are at an all-time high and when technological developments offer a staggering potential for Christian advance, religious strategists are beginning to revert to the most primitive of methods—open violence—to implant their views in society." [10] As *Christianity Today* points out elsewhere, "The primary task of the churches seems to have become something other than the proclamation of good news." [11]

On the one hand, demonstrations are sometimes used in a disruptive way to bring about a socially harmful result. On the other hand, say some evangelicals, they can be used to bring about a beneficial result when used within the law.

In each demonstration there are many factors to consider, so they should not be dismissed as being all of an identical set of ingredients. This can be seen as *Christianity Today* sums up the March on Montgomery:

The March to Montgomery is over, but the nation has not yet seen the end of large-scale public demonstrations which now serve as complex fronts for many ambitions. Legitimacy of public assembly and public protest against glaring social injustice are not the only issues involved in mass demonstrations. Communist sympathizers exploit these activities to undermine confidence in free-world governments. Selma was not without such entanglements . . . Political agitators exploit mob-ocracy to overthrow constitutional government rather than to achieve political reforms by traditional processes. Church leaders use demonstrations to identify the theologically confused and evangelistically dormant Church not only with social concern but also with specific legislative programs.[12]

In the above excerpt are these words: "Church leaders use demonstrations to identify the theologically confused and evangelistically dormant Church not only with social concern but also with specific legislative programs."

The terms *theologically confused* and *evangelistically dormant* are all too exact, yet true. Another sad truth is that there is a spurious social concern, because true social concern cannot exist where sound doctrine does not flourish. (This is a reference to the kind of social concern a Christian should have, and is no attack on social concern in general.) Christian social concern is born of accurate theological awareness. It is infused with yearning for the deliverance of the disadvantaged multitudes from any suffering which can possibly be alleviated. It *may* concern itself with specific legislative programs, but such programs will not be substitutes for concurrent direct aid evangelical churches might give when possible. Nor will they be legislative programs contrary to sound doctrine.

Can we say that evangelicals ought not to be concerned about political, social, and economic issues that cause hardship to people because then the gospel would be given second place to those issues? Such things can be put first and cause the gospel to be relegated to second place, but they need not be put first. Many evangelicals in the past and present have put the gospel first and because of this have been best able to understand and take proper action on other issues. To them, gospel primacy has meant an obligation to keep aware of urgent needs of people in all aspects of their lives, so as to direct God's Word to those areas and to be of the kind of practical help God enjoins, as we shall see.

The Christian and Protests

Can Christians take part in demonstrations and less organized protests? As discussed above, some evangelicals say they can under some circumstances.[13] A demonstration may be little more than a public stand against something manifestly evil, or it may be similar to some united labor or neighborhood action, strike-connected or not. It might be uniting with neighbors to petition for a traffic light, sometimes including standing at the needy corner. So much depends on the nature of the issues involved and the attitudes of those who take action. Perhaps the Christian may be called upon to stand with his community against some outrage. Taking a stand is a form of demonstration.

Again, some evangelicals say that Christians can never take part in demonstrations. They think of demonstrations, marches, picketing, as evils in themselves.

Because so many present-day social action operations have characteristics unacceptable to the evangelical, he does well to beware of participation.

One caution is necessary: The Christian ought always to be alert to see the clear indication which God may give of the need for a Christian to take a stand for righteousness. As in all other areas of a Christian's walk, he is to walk in the Spirit and can be confident that God will guide Him by the same Holy Spirit in accordance with His Word. Certainly God is able to help the Christian live in "demonstration of the Spirit and of power." [14]

It is legally permissible as a part of our constitutional rights of free speech and assembly to *demonstrate* if this is done in accord with law, is carried out to inform, and to influence beneficial social change. This can be part of the process of changing law by acceptable means. In these days of social action, organizations of the legal profession have performed a service by defining limits of action.

Riots? The Christian's only place in a riot is in attempting to minister spiritually and physically to the maimed as well as to the physically whole, difficult though this might be under such stressful situations.

Note comparisons of demonstrations (expressing dissent in open protest) and riots (extreme forms of civil disobedience) in the following excerpt from the Newsletter of the American Council on Education, in which the then President of the American Bar Association, Earl F. Morris, says: "I define civil disobedience as the open, wilful breaking by an individual or a group of a law which that individual or group believes to be unfair or unjust with a view toward effecting its change, or the committing of a similarly unlawful act in order to influence government policy. Contrasted with civil disobedience are dissent and protest, both of which are lawful means of disagreement. Dissent is the legal expression of one's concurrence with a generally prevailing opinion, usually by means of the spoken or written word; while protest is the legal expression of objection, disapproval or opposition, more often in the form of some type of action . . . ." [15]

It is generally the evangelical position (with exceptions) that the Christian should not engage in civil disobedience; dissent and protest could be expressed in ways that are not civil disobedience.

Political revolution is civil disobedience in its most violent form. Evangelicals do not revolt, however. Some evangelicals would make exceptions of instances in which governing powers usurp the prerogatives of God. The question is, *when* is this clearly evident? There are those Christians who say that revolution is permissible when government usurps the prerogatives of God in not meeting extreme and basic needs of the people. They point to the American Revolution in which some of the colonists engaged in civil disobedience, protesting against oppression, such as taxation without representation.

Some blacks and other minority group members are saying that the United States government of today is guilty of the same kind of abuses which separated our country from Great Britain. The Declaration of Independence [16] speaks of equality, of inalienable rights given all men by God, and of the government's responsibility to secure these rights to their people. Critics of our government point to that part of the Declaration which declares it is "the Right of the People to alter or abolish" government that is tyrannical. Defenders of our government may point to frequent laws and programs to correct abuses, and correctly say there is no parallel between American government today and British government of 1776. Most Americans do not realize that frustration upon frustration caused by not having basic human needs met can cause deprived people to be unaware of benevolent thoughts and acts at high levels and more aware of what seems official neglect if not abuse.

Some Different Views of Civil Disobedience

The layman, uninitiated in the intricacies of political, legal, and social philosophy, is understandably confused by the charges and countercharges concerning rebellion, denial of rights, and as to whether or not civil disobedience or violence are permissible. An excerpt from the address by Earl F. Morris, quoted earlier, reveals some of the important points which make broad generalizations unwise. Another factor which he portrays is that which shows acts of civil disobedience to be categorized in at least three ways: they are (1) illegal; or (2) a means of strife to gain the ends of agitators; or (3) the only possible means of protest to draw attention of the authorities to the plight of the neglected.

Dr. Morris says that peaceful civil disobedience was practiced in the early 1960s which became the "starting point for many changes in statutory law and case law and for the emergence of a new attitude toward the Negro on the part of the white community." [17]

Dr. Morris goes on to say that the protest march from Selma to Montgomery was protest and not civil disobedience, because it was permitted by a Federal Court and had to do with so basic a right as the right to vote. Some sit-ins, Dr. Morris adds, were necessary to test the validity of public accommodations laws by breaking the law, and by causing a test case, and were "a type of civil disobedience that is consistent with our legal order." [18] Some other sit-ins were disobedience without test case characteristics and, thus, not justifiable.

The following quotation from Dr. Morris' address includes discussion of rights, protests, and law with a combination of other factors:

Just as we approach anarchy when an individual may decide for himself which laws are "good" and which are "bad," we disrupt the foundation of the judicial process when an individual may determine without being subject to the charge of being civilly disobedient whether a law is Constitutional. I suggest that the state, too, is entitled to due process, and that any concept that goes beyond a true test case poses a threat to the legal order that should not be lightly accepted . . . .

When a group of college students marches on a campus in an orderly, peaceful fashion carrying anti-war signs, or when a university faculty member writes a paper criticizing the legality of the American position in Viet Nam, this is dissent—legal, Constitutional, protected by the first Amendment. But when students obstruct the work of interviewers representing the C.I.A., the Armed Forces and certain private corporations; or when students storm the Vice President of the United States in his car, hit the windows and body of the car with their fists and shout obscenities, this is civil disobedience in its most virulent form, and it is unlawful . . . .

What the persons who participate in these lawless acts seem to have forgotten is that, though their techniques might be effective for the moment, they are self-defeating because they endanger the same individual freedom they are intended to manifest . . . .

The concept of civil disobedience has been distorted in these times to justify violence and anarchy . . . .

These people misdirect and misrepresent the philosophy of dissent and the doctrine of civil disobedience. They are not attempting to change a law or influence government policy; . . . many of those who engage in civil disobediences today seem to be demanding for themselves the unlimited right to disobey laws . . . .

In our society, the rule of law serves as a basis for all social action. . . . Perhaps the most significant application of the rule of law—and surely the most timely in our present context—is the concept that each of us must comply with the law if we are to have an ordered society in which rights and responsibilities are concomitants . . . .

Whatever the attempted rationalizations to justify civil disobedience, whatever the claims for its necessity throughout our history, we have reached a point in the life of our nation when there arises an imperative need for the full acceptance of the rule of law as an essential doctrine and for the rebirth of civil obedience.[19]

According to the above, civil disobedience as properly conceived is part of the legal process by which laws may be tested, but it is being abused by those who misuse such a legal doctrine as part of their seeming to demand "for themselves the unlimited right to disobey laws."

There is a difference, then, between making a clamor by which multitudes seek recognition as human beings, and making a deliberate act of disobedience by which dissidents engage in fomentation of violence as part of a pattern of anarchy.

References for Chapter 7

1. Charles Evers, appearance on CBS/TV Program, "Face the Nation," quoted in the *Philadelphia Inquirer* (July 8, 1968).
2. Handlin, *Fire-Bell*, pp. 6, 7.
3. Ramsey Clark, Remarks addressed to Delegation of Poor People's Demonstrators, reported in the *Philadelphia Inquirer* (June 5, 1968).
4. See Martin Luther King, *Why We Can't Wait* (New York, Harper and Row, 1963).
5. Editorial, "The Rising Tide of Violence," *Christianity Today*, Vol. XI, No. 22 (August 18, 1967), p. 29.
6. Hebrews 12:14.
7. Panel discussion, "The Church and Social Concern," *Christianity Today*, Vol. XI, No. 14 (April 14, 1967), p. 6.
8. Frank E. Gaebelein, "The March to Montgomery," *Christianity Today*, Vol. IX, No. 14 (April 9, 1965), p. 46.
9. Editorial, "Too Bad About Detroit," *Christianity Today*, Vol. XII, No. 4 (Nov. 24, 1967), p. 24.
10. *Ibid.*, p. 25.
11. Editorial, "Putting First Things Second," *Christianity Today*, Vol. XII, No. 11 (March 1, 1968), p. 27.
12. Editorial, *Christianity Today*, Vol. IX, No. 14 (April 9, 1965), p. 32.
13. Clouse, et al., *Protest and Politics*, p. 141.
14. 1 Corinthians 2:4.
15. Address, American Council on Education, Earl F. Morris, President, reported in *Higher Education and National Affairs*, American Council on Education, Vol. XVII, No. 148 (April 19, 1968), p. 6.
16. United States Declaration of Independence, July 4, 1776.
17. Earl F. Morris, *loc. cit.*
18. *Idem.*
19. *Ibid.*, pp. 6, 7.

8

Treatment of the Poor

Civil Rights, Individual and Collective

So often, we are called upon to consider the *rights* of individuals.

Excerpts from the pen of Robert Linder illuminate the crucial aspects of civil rights:

In this decade civil rights has become the single most important domestic political issue in the United States as well as one of the burning moral and social issues confronting American Christians. The tragedy is that a cause so obviously righteous in both the political and religious sense should have become an issue at all for most Americans and/or Christians. But it has, and the complexities of the present situation need to be discussed and Christians need to be brought to grips with their political, social, and spiritual responsibilities in this matter . . . .

What are civil rights? The meaning should be obvious; the term is almost self-explanatory. Civil rights are simply those rights and liberties possessed by the individual citizen as a member of the state. In the case of the United States, they are those rights guaranteed to *all* Americans by the Bill of Rights and certain other amendments to the Constitution. Positive legislation by Congress also seeks to guarantee certain liberties to the individual against encroachment by other individuals or groups or even the central government. An example of this would be recent national and state laws in which individuals or groups are forbidden to discriminate against other individuals or groups because of their race, color, religion, or membership in labor unions.

In short, civil rights are those political, economic, and social rights guaranteed to all Americans by the Constitution and local, state, and federal legislation . . . .

The morality of slavery was only one of several issues leading to the Civil War, but for the churches it was the fundamental question. The scars of the great conflict of the last century are yet visible in American Protestantism and the basic question of whether it is sinful and immoral to deny other human beings their basic rights lingers on to the present . . . .

When one considers the relative positions of the whites and the blacks for two hundred and forty years prior to emancipation, it should not be surprising that it has taken nearly one hundred years to make fissures in the walls of mores and customs of so many people. When all of this became complicated by political, social, and prestige factors following the war, the way to understanding and reconciliation became even more elusive. And, of course, there was the continuing problem of changing the hearts of men, for at the root of the difficulties which have been experienced in gaining for all Americans their constitutional rights is the cold, hard fact of human perversity. The real obstacles to civil rights are usually not material but mental and spiritual, that is, they relate to what the Christian would call *sin*.[1]

Linder accurately speaks of the basic mental and spiritual elements involved today in social crises, and of the "continuing problem of changing the hearts of men." The Christian knows the spiritual issues well, usually, but does he sense accurately the mental and emotional crises as well? There is nothing so needed in establishing good relations with the poor as to understand their feelings, needs, rights. Many observers fail to understand poverty and the poor simply because they do not have much awareness that the people have feelings, aspirations, hopes, just as other people do—unless those are so stifled by frustrations that they are to a large extent lethargic and numb under the blight of unfulfilled needs and unused potential.

The matter of *rights* is of prime concern. Most of us are very zealous to protect our own rights and to point to the Bill of Rights and other safeguards in our United States Constitution. We are very upset if our rights are tampered with. Ought we not to be upset also if our poor neighbors are denied their rights?

A *right* is an individual liberty which each citizen has or is entitled to have. If citizens do not have rights because laws prevent them from doing so, the laws need to be changed in order to guarantee their rights. If there is as yet no law to implement their rights being honored or established, legislation should be instituted.

Whether or not we disapprove civil disobedience for any reason, can we not at least understand the plight of any citizens who are prevented from going through normal channels to call the attention of the authorities to their needs? We do not even have to resort to some implication that they may have tried through proper channels to get help in this way but were refused—although in too many instances this has been the case. Protesters might not be able to afford to go through expensive— prohibitively expensive—litigation, by way of overcrowded court dockets, to get attention to individual or group rights. Or, they may not even be aware that they *could* seek legal redress.

Our intention as evangelicals is not to be bogged down in endless haggling from one side to another of civil rights disputes, although there are times when we should take a stand on one side or another in a specific instance. Let the evangelical get at the heart of the matter. If people are deprived of food, education, health, employment and acceptance as equals with other human beings, to the extent to which they are neglected or abused, their rights are being infringed upon. As Oscar Handlin says, "No one, no matter how fortunate, can feel secure in rights that are denied to some." [2] As our society denies civil rights to some, to that extent our own enjoyment of civil rights is unfair unless we do whatever is possible to remove the discrimination.

Two consequences of a civil rights clash can be expected. Ordinarily, the clash ends in the quelling of the disorder. Then there is the period of adjustment afterward.

Along with the quelling of the disorder there should be persistent correction of human inequalities that caused the eruption. Along with the period of adjustment there should be mutual growth of understanding on the part of both sides as each side sees the other side's position in a calmer light. This leads to more amicable relationships which lead to at least a beginning degree of cooperation. Is it too much to say that in most of the present types of disorders the parties on both sides might all have some rights? That negotiations honestly entered into should protect the rights of all concerned and issue in better living together?

What we *cannot* condone is deliberate and purposely fomented lawlessness. We do not here refer to tests of the legality of laws or to spontaneous outbreaks which communicate evidence of social systems strains and of lack of provision for human needs. People who clamor for their rights often have not paid attention to understanding and living up to their responsibilities under the law. There is in such instances little awareness that law is best changed by recourse to the ballot box or to established legal process.

Our thoughts revert to the large majority of protesters in ghetto uprisings. They are not anarchistic, militant, criminal. They are simply poor. If authorities have not troubled themselves to anticipate and provide for survival needs and for living conditions with minimum adequacy and decency, the poor are in desperate straits. Present hunger and unemployment cannot be effectively cured by long and tortuous recourse to law, even if the individuals affected had means to take such steps.

When anyone sees that extreme needs (as for food, shelter, and work) cannot possibly be met by waiting for referenda and elections and changes in laws, what action can he take to help his neighbor? He is still his brother's keeper [3] and he is supposed to do unto others as he would have them do unto him [4] were he poor and without *connections* to speak for himself.

A citizen should seek new laws for old if regulations and laws obstruct the vital flow of human services to people in dire circumstances. This is not interference with legal process, but a part of it. It is a role of advocacy in which any proper influence is brought to bear to shape laws more and more to become the instruments of help to the people, as the true intent behind good laws actually is.

This is no mere academic matter. Note the words of Earl Johnson, Jr., "But in a nation dedicated to the ideal of justice before the law . . . it is inexcusable to permit discrimination on the basis of poverty in our legal system . . . . To my mind one of the very basic causes of civil disorder is the fact that as to many of the grievances held by the poor, there exist no legal peaceable mechanisms for redress, or if a mechanism exists, it is available only to those with financial means. Normally, the absence of a formal grievance procedure does not harm the more privileged classes to the degree it does the poor. The wealthy and to a lesser but still substantial degree, the middle class, can obtain redress through the exercise of informal power and influence." [5]

An evangelical Christian should be well-informed on major social issues so as to enter into discussion with his fellow Americans in a way that might help them understand the poor and other victims of social problems. An example of an issue that is much discussed today is that of capital punishment. This example is appropriate because both Christians and non-Christians differ among themselves about it; it has strong overtones of discrimination against the poor; financial power is brought to bear in a manipulative way; and it is soon to be ruled on by the United States Supreme Court.

Evangelicals are represented on a continuum anywhere from the extreme of opposing capital punishment to the extreme of endorsing it, and several positions between the extremes. Let us suppose that one particular evangelical favors capital punishment and is confronted by a person who is completely ignorant of what the Scriptures teach. The dialogue could go much like this:

The inquirer who asks what the evangelical believes about capital punishment might be surprised to learn that the evangelical is in favor of capital punishment. He might hear the reasons with accompanying Scripture passages and depart in strong opposition, leaving the evangelical puzzling over the unexpected rebuff. Wasn't he giving God's Word? Surely this was a case of rejection of God's truth.

What the evangelical might not realize is that he himself was unconsciously a stumbling block. He had not learned ahead of time what is commonly accepted by such an inquirer, nor bothered to ask him to give his reasons for not accepting capital punishment. He did not know that one of the inquirer's reasons for being against capital punishment was that people with money for legal appeals, bribes, or other influence allegedly can get themselves out of death penalties, in many instances, whereas the poor, including minority group members, cannot escape—or very rarely do.

This is but one of the prime examples of the present time when the Bible believer needs to know how to broach the subject of the gospel to others unfamiliar with the gospel. It is one thing for people to reject God's Word because of their refusal of God's way. It is another thing to refuse it because representatives of God are ignorant of conditions around them and how they affect other people's lives. It would be better for the evangelical to know the alleged prevalence of objections to capital punishment, and then to know how to give the Scriptures in an informed way so as not to drive the other person away unintentionally. If the person is aware of the evangelical's knowledge of the issue discussed, his next inclination might be to enter into conversation on the most important issues of eternal life or death. If he sees in the Christian a person who is concerned enough about discrimination against the poor, he might be attracted to feel he was a person with understanding of eternal values as well.

In this same vein, it might be well to note that some of the evangelicals who oppose capital punishment want to keep the person alive, because, among other things, as long as there is life there is hope of repentance, conversion, and rehabilitation.

Mutual Rights and Responsibilities

There is a most central issue in all of today's context of social action and social change which is second only to that of the effect of human depravity on social relationships. It is an issue which exists insidiously under the surface of the outward black-white and poor-nonpoor polarizations of which we are aware. It is reflected in such words as these which a protagonist of one side or the other might say: "I am in favor of his having his rights, as long as he remembers his rights stop where mine begin." While it is true that legally and other ways there might be desires and outward action to compromise or to segregate, this is not enough. What *is* needed most is an attitude expressed as follows: "Let us realize that your basic human rights and mine are identical, our mutual needs are the business of both of us, and whatever differences we do have we submit to examination together. Whether we resolve some of these differences or decide to maintain some of them, we continue under one understanding that we are interdependent within one relationship which it is our purpose to improve together."

Rights of the Poor

Mitchell Ginsberg, veteran worker with people and former New York City Human Resources Administrator and as such a member of the Mayor's cabinet, speaks about the increasingly vocal poor: "This group (the poor) is no longer prepared to sit quietly by and be left out, to have others make decisions for them. They want to have . . . something substantial to say about being involved. They will demand it and they will not go away . . . there is altogether too much talk . . . as if . . . the basic problems of the people would go away. Well, they won't." [6]

It is not accurate to suppose that all pressures or all methods used by the poor to seek assistance and a voice are to be given blanket approval, any more than it is accurate to suppose that *any* group should be given such approval. What is meant by speaking of the rights of the poor at this point is that they know their needs and will take drastic action to demand their needs be met if they are not given proper consideration. This includes the right to be represented in the planning of what is to be done for them, and by use of their own people where possible for *delivery of service*.

Attorney Lewis F. Powell, Jr., strikes a similar note in the theme of closing the gap between the classes in our country: "The gap between the prosperous middle classes and the genuinely underprivileged—both white and black—must be narrowed. Many mistakes have been made in the past, and there is enough blame for all to share. But we have passed the point where recriminations and bitterness will solve problems. We must come to grips realistically with the gravest domestic problem of this century. . . . At the same time, we must avoid the mindless folly of appeasing and even rewarding the extremists who incite or participate in civil disobedience . . . those . . . are the enemies of social reform and of freedom itself. . . ." [7]

Authority Figures and the Poor

Looking further into the personalities with which many of the poor identify their plight, several can be noted who to them embody exploitation, discrimination, and outright oppression.

The policeman, to most people a representative of helpful security and control, is to some of the poor a symbol of a society that holds them in check in order that that society might continue past abuses. The individual policeman may or may not be personally offensive in the eyes of those who think of society this way, but he has this idea to overcome before he can even begin to be helpful to some of the poor.

Whether or not the fact of police disparagement by the people is a widespread condition, the fact of misbehavior on both sides confirms the fact that all men are sinners. The fact that the Commission on Civil Disorders found instances of police brutality confirms the contention that such a thing actually exists. [8] The *Report* also comments on one police attitude as representing the core of the problem in an observation which is made by other sources as well: "although local police forces generally regard themselves as public servants with the responsibility of maintaining law and order, they tend to minimize this attitude when they are patrolling areas that are heavily populated with Negro citizens. There, they tend to view each person on the streets as a potential criminal or enemy, and all too often that attitude is reciprocated. Indeed, hostility between the Negro communities in our large cities and the police departments is the major problem in law enforcement in this decade. It has been a major cause of all recent race riots." [9]

It is evident that some police treat some people differently than they would if they understood their cultural backgrounds and some of their customs. Fortunately, some police training programs are stepping up this side of the education of their personnel.

The shopkeeper often discriminates against the poor,[10] especially in the realm of food prices. The poor themselves notice this. Government officials know this.[11] The Commission on Civil Disorders documents it: "The fact that most of the merchants who operate stores in almost every Negro area are white immediately contributes to the conclusion among Negroes that they are exploited by white society. In this situation, exploitative practices flourish . . . While higher prices are not necessarily exploitative in themselves, many merchants in ghetto neighborhoods take advantage of their superior knowledge of credit buying by engaging in various exploitative tactics. . . . Such tactics affect a great many low-income consumers." [12]

The slum landlord is often involved in unscrupulous practices, rent gouging, and much more. He has come in for some of our attention before this.

Several representatives of the white middle-class values of the majority of American society are rejected to at least some degree by the poor, including many poor other than the blacks. The schoolteacher often comes in for much of this resistance.

Welfare workers are often disdained by the poor. One recent aspect of this has been compounded by racial discord. Dislike of workers has been intensified by the supposition that workers who use birth control information to curb procreation are trying to curb black power by preventing births of black infants.

Government and the Poor

The double fact is that (1) only one quarter of the eligible poor are recipients of public assistance funds, and (2) a major cause for discontent among the poor is that most of them get ten percent and more *below* the amount necessary to maintain a family at the minimally adequate level of health and decency according to the State in which they reside. This condition exists in all too many states. It is therefore not surprising that federal programs have bypassed regular channels in crash programs of the anti-poverty kind, which in turn have been greatly inadequate. Regardless of how much (and there is much) good is done by regular welfare programs and special programs like Community Action Programs, Job Corps, Youth Corps, Teacher Corps, Head Start, and so forth, the amount of money and of programs needed to help so large a number of people is very great—even beyond all these. Because of so many inadequacies in programs, or restrictions in them, many of the poor react in anger at them.

On the one hand, some of the poor do not avail themselves of assistance programs of which they have been informed. On the other hand, they are often left uninformed about rights, privileges, and material assistance to which they are entitled by law. An example of the latter is one which came to light at the beginning of 1970 in a county of an eastern state. Government food stamp programs were available for eighteen thousand of the poor but only two thousand were aware that they were entitled to such assistance.

Animosity against insufficient provisions through government programs, which were once the only help of many in Depression days, is largely because they have not been adjusted to fit the needs of the poor. It is also an animosity which can be played upon by those who agitate the poor to riot. Such agitators represent the government as the villainous conspirator against the people, keeping them in subjection by denying them the necessities of life.

In order here is another quotation from Dr. Ginsberg's lecture. He points to inadequacies in welfare programs, but comes to the heart of the issue as to how many of these come about: "We have not spoken up sufficiently about the inadequacies of welfare and other programs in our urban communities and in the rest of the United States. I am prone to say, because I believe it wholeheartedly, that welfare didn't cause this problem. Welfare picks up the casualties of other systems: the failures of education, of employment, of poor health, the results of segregation and discrimination. These systems fail and we wind up with the result, and then somehow it's our fault and we have all these people on welfare." [13]

Is it not clear that the Christian is obligated, privileged, to help the poor today? The Christian and his church should understand the poor as much as possible, so as to work with them when possible and help them to help themselves.

References for Chapter 8

1. Robert D. Linder, "A Christian Approach to the Contemporary Civil Rights Movement," in Robert G. Clouse, et al., *Protest and Politics*, pp. 122, 123, 126.
2. Handlin, *Fire-Bell*, p. 7.
3. Genesis 4:9, 10.
4. Matthew 7:12.
5. Office of Economic Opportunity, Legal Services Program, Earl M. Johnson, Jr., "Director's Column," *Law in Action*, Vol. 2, No. 11 (March, 1968).
6. Mitchell I. Ginsberg, "Changing Values in Social Work," First Ann Elizabeth Neely Memorial Lecture, 16th Annual Program Meeting, Council on Social Work Education, Minneapolis (January 26, 1968), *mimeographed*, p. 4.

7. Lewis F. Powell, Jr., "Civil Disobedience: Prelude to Revolution," address at Pt. Clear, Ala., October 5, 1967, reprinted in *U.S. News and World Report* (October 30, 1967), p. 69.

8. N.A.C.C.D., *Report,* pp. 10, 50, 64, 68, 81, 105, 116, 302 footnote.

9. *Ibid.,* p. 85.

10. David Caplovitz, *The Poor Pay More* (New York, The Free Press, 1963).

11. Phyllis Groom, "Prices in Poor Neighborhoods," Bureau of Labor Statistics Reprint No. 2506, in *Monthly Labor Review* (October, 1966), pp. 1085–1090.

12. N.A.C.C.D., *op. cit.,* pp. 274–276.

13. Ginsberg, *loc. cit.,* pp. 6, 7.

9

Peace and Youth

Other Precipitants of Social Action

We have discussed almost exclusively those social action issues which have stemmed from poverty and have involved the poor most directly. Not all crises originate among the poor.

There are grievances which flow from differences among people which are not racial differences but may be economic. Of the complex of factors, ideological and chronological components are distinguishable. As a result of these differences, antiwar and student demonstrations are in prominent evidence.

It is neither accurate nor sufficient to relegate these activities to the discord with the oversimplifications that antiwar activities are sinful opposition to government policy; that youth uprisings, campus revolts, hippie subcultures, and recourse to drugs are entirely due to the influence of subversives. They are in many instances due to such influences, but by no means only these. Agitators use real or fancied grievances which are springboards to incitement of crowds.

Among evangelicals there is practically every position represented, from opposition to war under any circumstances to defense of one's country in obedience to its leaders. It must be realized with equal clarity that evangelicals do not seek to evade the service of the country in wartime. They insist on service in some capacity. The status of conscientious objector is given to those who cannot, for the sake of their personal moral and religious convictions, bring themselves to bear arms. Such COs perform non-combatant tasks.

Conscientious objectors who are evangelical would, along with other evangelicals, oppose efforts by nonevangelicals to hinder the government's war effort. They would oppose attempts to escape personal participation in the conflict now raging in Viet Nam, as conscientious objectors or otherwise. Even the belief that this particular war is unjustified would not lead an evangelical to oppose his government, except by the ballot box in the prescribed way to change government policy. All this would not keep such a person from voicing disagreement, but this is not opposition.

The fact that wars are largely undeclared these days causes much of the confusion on this issue. It is a fact seized upon by some who argue that it is unjust to require youth to fight for some foreign nation's survival when no war exists officially. On the other side, there are those who insist the war ought to be openly declared, and all-out efforts made to bring it to a victorious conclusion. Between the two positions, a third is taking shape in which the goal is to withdraw from Viet Nam if and when military and political affairs make it possible to do so.

A youth today lives under the influence of impending doom. If he does not have the assurance of personal faith in Christ as Saviour, he has little hope in this life and none for the next. Without this faith, he does not know the strength of the fact that God is Sovereign and that complete destruction of the present creation (and its subsequent renewal) cannot take place except at the time prophesied in the Scriptures.

With the use of the first atomic bomb in 1945, people have come to fear physical extermination. This may not always be a conscious fear, but is always in the back of their minds. As opposition to war increases with greater intensity and frequency than during any former period in our history, this does not discount the nature of the waves of pacifism in the past. It is rather to say that all past reasons have climaxed in the present and more imminent fear of annihilation, practically on a world-wide scale. Ranging anywhere from an understandable protest against harm to loved ones by enemy action, through honest opposition to even a defensive war, to opportunistic and particularly vitriolic denunciation of American war efforts by subversives, the peace movement is with us.

Views of Government

We have opposition to our government in protests against harm done by our forces to soldiers and civilians on the enemy's side. Yet there is little or no dissatisfaction expressed by some peace groups against harm to our forces or our allies.

In the social action seen in some antiwar demonstrations, we see what might be called a *villain* idea of government. Some hold this view sincerely, others as a lever to use toward other objectives and as a means of influence over followers. It does not matter whether such views of government emanate from anarchistic or other roots; these views are extant in blatant form.

All too many Americans are ignorant of the development of true liberalism and democracy in England and America, which gives a more complimentary image of government. It is seen as arising by contract between rulers and the governed, and by consent of the latter. One factor for concern today is that even among government personnel, as well as other citizens, many have no idea of the historic American view of the beneficial intent and operation of government.

It would be unwise, however, to give blanket endorsement of

a particular government, merely because it is government. It is also in the British-American tradition that a government should be questioned on any course in which it appears to be pursuing the wrong policy. It would be wise therefore to look underneath the protests of antiwar demonstrators to see elements of valid concern, whether or not any of us agree personally with those particulars. Our space program is said to be necessary; yet should it not be of concern that so many of our public monies are spent in space programs when millions in our country and our world lack basic essentials of life? The present war may be of importance to our nation's survival; yet should it not be of concern to us that so many people, poor and nonpoor, of various racial and ethnic backgrounds, are dying in a war which to so many Americans seems unjust? These are but two of the questions asked sincerely by some, who are in some instances not opposed to war in general so much as they are opposed to this particular war.

"The Powers That Be"

While opposition and criticism directed at a particular administration may be permissible short of treason and within the bounds of legally permissible behavior, *government* is the basic concept to be defended here. All administrations are human and fallible, but insofar as they serve in the governing function they are to be honored and obeyed.

The Scriptures require us to have the attitude that submits to government. They tell us that "the powers that be are ordained of God." [1] The behavior commanded here even enjoins us to behave in such a way as to elicit approval by the government: "do that which is good, and thou shalt have the praise of the same." [2] If we decide that our government is not governing wisely, whether in prosecution of a war, or in helping people in ways in which they cannot help themselves, we in a democracy change our leadership by use of the ballot box.

In any event, we are to have just the opposite attitudes from that of a man heard by this writer who used extreme profanity coupled with the name of a President of the United States. The same Scripture context containing the verses quoted above tells us that the man who is in a place of political government over us is a minister of God for the good of the governed.[3] As such, he is entitled to honor, not profanity.

Aside from the right to change governments by peaceful means, the obligation of the Christian is to be submissive to the powers over him because resistance to government is resistance against God. "Whosoever therefore resisteth the power, resisteth the ordinance of God: and they that resist shall receive to themselves judgment." [4]

It would appear, then, that the Christian, while he may have a different opinion from that of the President, must at least assume that the President is in a better position than he to know whether or not a particular conflict is justifiable as vital to our nation's survival. The President would not be hesitant to resist armed attack upon us, even if opponents accused him of using violence. Perhaps at times "violence seems right. Who will claim that Hitler should have been allowed to go unopposed?" [5] Likewise we may contend that to whatever extent a war is comprised of fellow citizens defending our very persons instead of ourselves and our families doing so in person, such a war is justifiable.

It should be noted that even the best of governments are composed of human beings. We ought to examine the acts of our governments to see if they are discharging their duties as "powers ordained of God" should do. Too naïve and uncritical an attitude toward government led some Christians in Germany to give unwitting approval to the Nazi government's slaughter of Jews simply because it was government policy. This brought great embarrassment when realized to be so great an error.

The Experience of Peace

Whether in time of turmoil or of comparative calm, the Christian himself is told to pray that peace may prevail for the better prosecution of his own religious duties and evangelization of the lost.[6] He notices also that Jesus did not object to the disciples' owning swords [7] for defensively useful purposes. He notices, above all, that peace is a matter of spiritual dimension, compared to which the presence or absence of outer wars is of lesser importance. They who know Him who "is our peace" [8] can best serve God and country by getting people to know God's peace through Him. People who do not have any inner peace with God because they do not have faith in Christ as personal Saviour do not realize what they are missing. They do not have the peace of God to keep their hearts and minds through Christ Jesus.[9] We who *do* know this peace of God should be even more concerned about wanting to restore peace in our time so that they who do not know Christian life through Christ may have an opportunity to enjoy temporal peace as much as possible. The more peace that prevails, the greater our opportunities to get the gospel of salvation out to others, from the standpoint of facility of travel and communications facilities in disseminating the Message.

The absence of the Christian's inner peace from the lives of those who have not yet come to know Him is touched upon by Billy Graham: "Looking on our American scene, Jesus would say: 'Beware of covetousness, beware of the spirit of perpetual discontent with what life offers, forever wanting more, forever looking at other people's conditions in life and never being content.'" [10] It is apparent, then, that outer striving for peace in the world is good if properly done, because God recommends a peaceful environment. On the other hand, where Christ is absent from the heart, inner discontent goads many to agitate for outward peace in an attempt to substitute that outward peace for the inner reality that God wants to give. The Christian ought to recommend both outward peace in society as God pleases to permit it and God's inner peace as well.

The Apostle Paul speaks of learning to live in contentment even when living under adverse circumstances: "I have learned, in whatsoever state I am, therewith to be content." [11] This does not mean, à la Marx, that religion is an opiate which keeps the person helplessly under the heel of those who would exploit him. It does mean that the Christian, under whatever kind of government he lives, finds the Lord to be his sufficiency. This, a non-Christian should seek.[12] A Christian's reaction to oppression of himself and others should be to remove the oppression through proper channels. Yet he is still content in Christ, whatever his circumstances, because he has all of God's spiritual resources available to draw upon.[13]

The Economic Base of Protests

The study of protests should be viewed in historical perspective at this point: George Romney, then governor of Michigan, remarked that black power advocates reminded him to "look how labor has organized to get power. . . ." [14] The obvious implication is that such advocates were patterning their activities after what labor did in the last one hundred years, which is to organize and use strikes and pickets and marches with new variations to fit local circumstances. This is some reflection of the fact that the uprisings we see, whether over racial issues or peace or youth demands, have heavy economic bases either as to cause or goal or both.

In our American economy there will be periodic outbreaks of civil disorders and subsequent attempts to legalize whatever aspects of the outbreaks can be tolerated. This kind of legalization happened in the legal sanctioning of picketing and some kinds of strikes.

Christians then and Christians now have had much travail of conscience over what kinds of agitation they can engage in, even if legalized, in the light of the scriptural injunction to be content. It is not that the Christian does not want improvement of personal circumstances or of those of his neighbors. He does not, however, want to go along with the covetous spirit of the age.[15]

When Samuel Gompers was asked what labor wanted, and he answered, "More," he set the keynote for some attitudes of labor (and many others) since. The Christian ought to champion those who need enough *more* to live on an acceptable plane at least of minimum adequacy and decency, and to disapprove of greedy grasping for covetousness' sake. Viewed as part of the latter, it is appalling that peace movements and some demonstrations ostensibly to help the poor can be manipulated into being tools and fronts for those who want power and the wrong kind of *more*. Above all, Christians should insist in conversation with others that whether or not they get *more* or have less, God will do for them and the ones to whom they speak exactly what God has been doing through the centuries: God will keep in perfect peace those who truly serve Him, because their minds are stayed on Him.[16] Their treasure is laid up in heaven and not on earth.[17]

Youth

There is so much written about youth today and about their behavior that it is easy to see that many of our American people have failed to understand many of our youth.

While other results have stemmed from banning the use of the

Bible as a part of worship in public schools, one major result
for children and youth from Bible-believing homes is that they
do not have devotions in any form during school hours.

Parents of many of our youth have forsaken use of the Bible
in their homes, and relegated spiritual leadership to the churches.
Many of the churches no longer believe Jesus to be God, reject
the Bible as the divinely inspired Word of God, and have
relinquished control of the youth to the state-controlled schools.

The schools have in turn lost hold of youth, especially in the
instances of colleges once founded to honor God and educate
youth in Christian ways for Christian service. We have as a
nation taught in our schools many moral standards which have
their roots in the Scriptures, but we have forsaken the Scriptures
as the rule by which all conduct must be measured.

We have not carefully given the Scriptures to the youth to
reinforce the moral standards which are still largely contained
in the laws of the land and which were originally based on the
Scriptures to a large extent. We are seeing in youth's unrest a
logical progression from several generations before them, each
of which has more and more openly forsaken imposed standards
not justified in their minds because the Word of God has not
been adequately explained to them.

Youth rebel against hypocritical self-righteousness of some of
their elders which is evident in the absence of holy and ethical
living. They reject the shams of this kind and look askance at
the absorption of their elders with material gain and worldly
status.

In addition, we are reaping the results of our rejection of our
youth. Children under agrarian society values were wanted,
needed, if only to provide enough workers for family farm or
business. Today, many families are prone to look upon children
as a liability whose care must be provided for only until they

are launched out and away from the parents—as soon as possible. Many children feel more and more rejected as parents become increasingly engrossed in their own pursuits. Economic demands force many mothers to work, and this cuts down time which mothers spend with their children.

Another large element in the effect of our complex society on youth is a problem called *anomie* (standardlessness). The youth are confused by having so many standards successively or concurrently presented to them, and by which they are expected to live. Standards promulgated by the home, the school, the church, the military, the peer group, the neighborhood subculture, may cause grave conflict and resultant confusion.

There are also many indications that youth especially resent lack of personal attention by college faculty. Impersonal college experience, along with the pressures of high educational and occupational standards and the realities of economic pressures, give some clue as to why some of our youth feel they will explode if they do not seek some kind of escape. Those of our youth who are not in personal fellowship with Christ all too often seek escape in drugs, vagabond-like wanderings, sex, and even violence.

Above all else, so many youth have not been given the opportunity even to consider the claims of Christ on their lives. They have not been given the opportunity of *belonging* to Him. The predicament of so many of them is like that of the young Christian who recently had a battle with narcotics. When confronted with 1 Corinthians 6:19, 20, she said, "I never realized that even my body belongs to him!"

References for Chapter 9

1. Romans 13:1.
2. Romans 13:3.
3. Romans 13:4.
4. Romans 13:2 (New Scofield Reference Edition of the Bible).

5. Fred A. Alexander, "The Day of the Evil Gun," *Freedom Now* (July–August, 1968), p. 4.
6. 1 Timothy 2:1, 2.
7. Luke 22:38.
8. Ephesians 2:14; Romans 5:1; Acts 10:36; Isaiah 53:5.
9. Philippians 4:7.
10. Billy Graham, *World Aflame* (Garden City, Doubleday and Co., 1965), p. 184.
11. Philippians 4:11.
12. 2 Corinthians 9:8.
13. 1 Corinthians 3:21–23.
14. George Romney, Address on the economic plank of the Party platform, 29th Republican National Convention, Miami Beach, Florida (August 8, 1968).
15. Luke 12:15.
16. Isaiah 26:3, 4.
17. Matthew 6:19–21.

PART II

Evangelical Christian Social Action

(Past, Present, Future)

10

Social Action and Social Change

Suspended Animation

As we turn from social action in general and focus more closely upon evangelical action, we address ourselves to a first question: What has caused the suspended animation of the evangelicals in the areas of helping people in tangible, temporal, material needs? In the remainder of this study we will be examining the question to whatever extent the answers will help us move forward in such ministries.

The evangelical Christian today looks at social action and disapproves of much of it because it is violent, not in accustomed channels, and often in behalf of causes he does not feel he can endorse.

Even when social action is to him an acceptable kind and in connection with causes he can approve, other people are often doing the helping and he is not!

What has made the evangelical largely forsake open-air ministries and other aggressive attempts to contact large groups of people when possible, indoors or out? There are several answers to this, but one thing is certain. Evangelicals, to all too large an extent, have not kept in touch with the multitudes. We can explain much of this lapse, but we cannot justify its continuance any longer.

Social Change

Along with social action, social change is another term which is being featured by constant use in today's milieu. Social change is a continual process, taking place in society by the very nature of the dynamic which works in society. This dynamic is characterized by interaction of people; people are constantly changing.

Social action and social change are closely related and intertwined. Social action causes social change of a more rapid kind than probably would have taken place without being precipitated by social action efforts. Social change sometimes brings about social action. As used in this paragraph, social action and social change are allusions to action and change brought about by conscious effort of human beings to bring about such change purposely. The use of these terms is different from but not in conflict with the use of these same terms to denote sociological processes. The core of this use is in the question as to whether or not a desired change in society would take place by automatic process without the insertion of purposeful social action.

People change. In one sense, social action may be thought of as insertion into the lives of people those factors which would cause changes in the lives of people, causing different changes than would have taken place without such factors. It does not matter whether or not we say that the social action of dissatisfied groups does or does not bring about special change. What matters is that we be careful not to dismiss all social action movements under the mistaken impression that they are all temporary or intrusive efforts. Some of them will, upon scrutiny, prove to be strong acceleration of regular and valid change to speed up the closing of the gap between normal functioning of society and its malfunctions. Other social action movements will vanish from the scene after opportunistic and abortive operations. Yet others will prove opposed to constructive change and may foster detrimental outcomes. It is necessary that we treat normal and abnormal change with the same discernment of the basic values of valid human need present in each situation.

The community in which the problems occur must move to bring about needed change. It does so through identifying the needs which cause the problems. It adopts social policies by which to work toward goals it sets. The implementation of the policies is social action by which the desired social changes are brought about. Before the popular concept of social action in the forefront of attention today, *this* is what has been understood to be social action, through community organization processes. This is an orderly and reasoned procedure and is every bit as much entitled to be called social action as most hasty and precipitous social action of our day.

On the other hand, social policy and social planning have failed to produce much needed social action in the traditional way to such an extent that people in need are goaded into action. Justifiably or not, and prodded by the inroads of the *big four*, many of our poor are giving warning that legitimate social action by political and social welfare authorities must accelerate social change, or major antagonistic disruptions will continue and increase.

The Christian and Planned Social Change

It should be self-evident that evangelical Christians ought to be interested in change as God brings it about in people. Too often we leave it to Him without realizing He wants us to be His channels through which He brings about change in us and in others through us. Although it is true that we ought not to mimic the world just because the world is doing something and we want to do it also, we should nevertheless take note that the business world and the professional world make deliberate plans to *bring about change.*

Much is being written today about planned social change. One of the texts used to facilitate planned change contains these words: "if we are to maintain our health and a creative relationship with the world around us, we must be actively engaged in change efforts directed toward our material, our social, and spiritual environments." [1]

Evangelicals ought to have a strong motivation to bring about planned change, to be "actively engaged in change efforts." God has *planned change* for those whose lives he changes. He chooses Christians as agents to convey the change-producing message. It is sad if the world is in many instances straining every nerve to bring about improvement in itself, and Christians often seem to have no interest in being agents of immediate as well as eternal change. The Lord Jesus has a penetrating remark in the Sermon on the Mount: "What do ye more than others?" [2] We might safely suppose that He wants us to strain every nerve to spread the soul-changing Word to as many souls as can be reached, so that God Himself can thereby bring about change. [3] Today, even more than ever, this means using Christian social action along with evangelism.

We do not mix gospel and works of helpfulness to people in need. The two, evangelism and social action, are separate methods, used together. It is not merely a matter of semantics to insist that these are separate methods. It is of vital doctrinal significance to make clear that good works flow out from a life that has been changed, not by social action, but by the gospel, the evangel.

The renewed soul, the Christian *born from above,* must be grounded in sound doctrine beginning at conversion. This sound doctrine, more than ever before, must point out that he has been saved in order to carry out God's program of good works.[4] There are so many such works that can be profitable (helpful) to men! [5]

Social Change Pressures

Just as the idea of social action today conjures up the image of wronged people taking steps to correct the evils afflicting them, social change is thought of as the process of accomplishing the specific reform sought. Pressure is one characteristic of social action, which in turn causes social change.

One illustration of sustained pressure causing major social change may be taken from history. A rough but significant parallel to what is occurring today is the instance of the comparative European peace, which existed from 1815 to 1914. By 1914, many irresistible pressures had destroyed the sociopolitical balance of power that had lasted ninety-nine years. Many adjustments took place in the years immediately following. In similar fashion, so many pressures have existed in our nation which were built up from 1863 and before, in connection with the acceptance of the Negro. The balance of tension has been altered so that the black American is beginning to experience in fact many of the freedoms previously promised and legislated. Christian social action today includes having the right attitudes toward black progress when it is true progress. It also includes Christian action on the blacks' behalf as this becomes possible.

Cultural pluralism is one conceptual ingredient of the past status quo which has come in for sharp reassessment. It is one thing for freedom to include the right of people to maintain their own group identity and customs in the midst of the larger body politic composed of many diverse groups. It is another thing for a dominant culture to consider itself superior to rather than equal with smaller cultures living with it. Equality is in our national documents, but not always in our national deportment.

America must at all costs accelerate sincere implementation of the spirit of cultural pluralism, with true equality of intent and performance.

Some views of society, rather than emphasizing factors which unify, emphasize differences and separation caused by differences. Differentiation is itself a social process which takes place within society without conscious effort on the part of the people involved, and is neither good nor bad in itself.

Differentiation, then, is one thing. Causing differences is a particular kind and part of differentiation. In the name of democratic process, it is often insisted that a person take one side or another on racial or other key issues. Suggestion that a person *stand up and be counted*, ordinarily a mark of democratic identity with a common cause, is often resulting in polarization rather than collaboration.

In these days—when it is being affirmed by one side that the American dream and the melting pot process are still valid views of what is happening, and that we are merely going through further stages in their realization; and the other side is saying that they are exploded views which are proven so by social upheaval today—the Christian has a duty. He is to stand for beneficial social change.

Taking the Christian Stand

It should not be thought that Christians are averse to taking a stand. The Christian is, in one sense, taking a stand for God in any conflict insofar as his purpose is to represent Christ to people on both sides of the conflict. He is much like a surgeon in a war zone ministering to the wounded regardless of their being friendly or hostile. The surgeon's attack is on the factors causing the physical anguish. The Christian's attack is against anything which threatens the spiritual or temporal well-being of his fellow men, regardless of the sides people are taking in civil strife.

The major question is, What constitutes evil in such circumstances? This is the issue: The Christian by nature takes a stand— a stand for God. When he is also obliged to defend some secondary cause, he must be sure it is one in which he can represent God first and in so doing stand in defense of his fellow men. Usually, if a cause is truly in defense of his fellows in the area of their basic needs, he will be found to be standing for God.

There is at last a climate today—as well as a dire need for our witness—which more than anything will force us to know present-day issues, and do something about them when possible. We can be *for the Lord* and also be concerned for the needs of others.

There is a climate which is passing from us and is being replaced by the new climate. In past decades, a Christian often fitted well into the evangelical's culturally placid scheme by being *only for the Lord* and leaving peripheral or worldly specifics to others. If a Christian spoke up for or against a controversial issue, politically, socially, economically, he was categorized by some fellow evangelicals as "sound" if he agreed with their particular position (if they had any position at all). He was "unsound" if he were different in position. To speak up in some circles meant for the Christian a sure identification by some people with Communists or the radical right or the new left or the socialists or (more recently) the "establishment" or against the "establishment" and so on and on.

This present hour gives us an opportunity to represent the Lord as much as evangelicals have done in other periods of opportunity in national crises. Only the most determined evangelical isolationists can henceforth for the "foreseeable" future justify noninvolvement in a helpful way in the burning issues of the day.

Ministering to the needs of mankind is a major part of our service to God. Planning how to minister is more and more going to have to include the planning and carrying out of evangelical Christian social action.

References for Chapter 10

1. Ronald Lippitt, Jeanne Watson and Bruce Westley, *The Dynamics of Planned Change* (New York, Harcourt, Brace and World, 1958), p. 3.
2. Matthew 5:47.
3. 2 Timothy 3:15–17.
4. Ephesians 2:10.
5. Titus 3:8.

II

Presuppositions and Moral Standards

An indispensable component of this study dictates that we assert now that our entire position is predicated on the revelation from God of His eternal Word, the Bible. From it we establish basic presuppositions, and upon those presuppositions we build the Christian position in accordance with the Word. This includes a position on social action.

Presuppositions

It is necessary to ascertain by what norms social problems are identified. The norms in turn are determined in the light of basic presuppositions.

A point at which to begin examining the presuppositions underlying the Christian view of the world is that of the unity of knowledge which proceeds from the all-wise God. There are those who would divide knowledge into two compartments, the sacred and the secular. This division may stem from a variety of sources. Perhaps it comes from an assumption that the pseudo-scientific views of evolutionists may condescend to share a divided house with traditional religious dogma. Or it may come from the separation often made between the *city of man* and the *city of God.* This artificial dichotomy may come from any combination of sources in which the human and the divine are set in apposition to one another, whether in conflict or not. It matters not, for instance, whether we blame Descartes or Aristotle or Zoroaster or whomsoever else. The idea of a dichotomy is with us just the same, and we must deal with it.

The Scriptures hold to no such dualism. Jesus Christ is Himself "the truth"; [1] "the power of God, and the wisdom of God"; [2] and "in him dwelleth all the fulness of the Godhead bodily." [3] It is as a part of God's process of revealing His plan of redemption through the work of Christ as Reconciler and Mediator that we see Christ manifested in order to bring back into unity of fellowship with God that creature, man, who had made two compartments, the holy and the sinful, when he sinned against God. By man's sin, true wisdom became obscured and man resists it yet by declaring there are two realms of wisdom—the sacred and the secular. When a person becomes reconciled to God by faith in Christ, he knows then that God has indeed but one wisdom. What human "Eye hath not seen, nor ear heard, neither have entered into the heart of man," [4] God assists the new Christian to understand.

Two basic presuppositions of the Christian world view are inherent here. These are the factors of (1) the non-Christian's inability to have God's spiritual discernment because of (2) the underlying factor of sin. Whereas the Christian has the key to understanding spiritual knowledge, the non-Christian cannot understand such knowledge because of the distortion caused by sin. Referred to as the *natural man,* the non-Christian "receiveth not the things of the Spirit of God: for they are foolishness unto him: neither can he know them, because they are spiritually discerned." [5] The way to have spiritual discernment is to be cleansed from sin through faith in Jesus Christ as Saviour, so as to have "the mind of Christ." [6]

There are those who imply that man has progressed from the

sacred to the secular. Such a view is enunciated by Harvey Cox in his argument that the Bible has actually helped liberate religious man from spiritual restriction and has assisted his secular orientation! One theme in his book, *The Secular City*, is to the effect that the secular is the inevitable evolution from the biblical, brought about by it and advanced from it.[7] Such a view degrades the Bible from an eternal to a temporal book, and useful for one major purpose in one epoch of man's development but not particularly outstanding otherwise.

The trouble with this view of Cox' is that the secular man lives his life within the too-restricted limits of his own experiences and perceptions. For the evangelical Christian, the merely secular view is much too small and incomplete. The *secular* parts of human experience for the Christian are transfigured by their true importance in God's economy. The secular, then, is not the zenith of man's development; it is, rather, transformed and given true meaning for spiritual men as they see it in the light of God's entire plan.

The Standard

These presuppositions of man's sin and inability to understand the truths of God in proper perspective lead us to look a little more closely at the nature of the Scriptures upon which these and other presuppositions of the Christian position are established.

In Proverbs we are told, "Where there is no vision, the people perish." [8] More exactly rendered, this says, "Where there is no God-given revelation, received, accepted, and put into practice, the people mill about in confusion." Where people do not know or have not lived according to God's standard there is confusion resulting from sin and accompanied by inability to understand God's truth.

Do riots and disorders trouble us? Frequently, riots and insurrections are not analyzed from the standpoint of their spiritual significance. They come in part from the fact that some of the people engaged in them have not had presented to them or have not accepted the clear standard of personal and social righteousness, the Bible. In the light of the inability of any man to see with spiritual eyesight unless his eyes have been opened by the process of the new birth,[9] how can we expect rioters or riot-breakers to see evil accurately when the truth of God which gives spiritual eyesight has not even been presented to them?

So attuned is the mind of the secular man to what he can see and touch that he looks at a major political upheaval and calls it a revolution. A deep-seated and revolutionary process of social change which may include some political ingredients is an even more formidable occurrence than the political realignment we call a revolution. Arnold M. Rose admits that a revolution, while usually occurring rapidly, does not always do so, and is not necessarily brought about by the use of violence.[10]

Looking at this from another angle, it is not a revolution in the fullest sense when we have what is often popularly called a *revolution* in cybernetics, in sex, in race relations, in weapons, in the condition of the poor. These major changes within a society and together with other major changes may cause or comprise a full social revolution. Sometimes even a political upheaval is not too revolutionary because it sometimes results in very little basic change in the social conditions and social structure in which it occurs.[11]

In preceding pages we have discussed demonstrations and riots and insurrections and civil disobedience and revolutions as outward strife. It would be incongruous to be able to identify such overt action and remain unaware of revolution in the sense in which we are discussing it here.

A far-reaching and total revolution is a change in most departments of a society, brought about by basic alterations in the structure of that society, affecting even the basic mores themselves which change from one set of mores to another during such a revolution. That there is a revolution of great depth taking place today is indicated by surface revolutions of the kind referred to above. The word *surface* is used because such revolutions are serious enough in their own right, but they are symptomatic of an even deeper condition. We are prone to fix attention on outward consequences and to fail to see deeper causes. If we are merely secularistic and have arbitrarily ruled out the sacred, we are all the more incapable of seeing the root cause. Many social ills stem from situations caused by sinful human behavior.

We are still suffering the consequences of the first and most significant revolution, that of man against God in Eden, as a result of which all men are sinners and liable to punishment for sin. What was the climax point of the first major revolution? Was it not when Satan said to our first parents, "Yea, hath God said?" [12]

New Morality and Old Morality

The general revolution against God has shown itself in the rejection of biblical morality. One cause of some social problems and of some social action which causes yet more problems is the espousal of another form of rejection of Bible standards referred to as the *new morality*. Wirt lists several ethical positions which are contrary to the biblical ethic.[13] He points out that the new morality is not really a new position, but has come to the fore in the last decade.

Solomon tells us that there is nothing new under the sun. It is nothing new for leaders in any generation to reapply some ethic which has been used in former times, to give particular justification to behavior on the current scene.

Many religious leaders have failed to be faithful proclaimers of God's truth and have therefore had no weapon against resultant moral and spiritual degeneracy. Since most such leaders do not accept or use God's standards as absolute law in their own behavior, they are powerless to communicate them to their parishioners so that they in turn might know how to cease from violations of biblical personal ethical standards. These leaders have resurrected and reapplied under the name *new morality* an ethic, a form of overindulgent casuistry, which is deadening and salving to the conscience. It is a frantic face-saving device to lend ecclesiastical permission to much that deserves nothing but scriptural denunciation with a call for repentance and forsaking of sin. J. Milton Yinger admits this in part. While he is not speaking of the *new morality* as such, he says that there is a process of adjustment: "what is often called secularization today is the inevitable adjustment of the church to dramatic changes in the world within which it works." [14] If by adjustment Yinger means the understanding of people and their needs so as to minister to them the better without compromise of principles, this is one thing. If compromising God's standards is done, that is another, and the very thing done under new morality attitudes.

The *new morality* is enthronement once again of man's conscience as his authority. That conscience is magnified by the situation ethicists is seen in Joseph Fletcher's words: "Facing forward toward moral choices yet to be made, conscience makes decisions." [15] Situation ethicists purport to honor the Bible, but do not consider it binding if conscience deems a course of action contrary to the Scriptures to be more expedient in a given situation.

The conscience is not dependable apart from submission to divine standards. This should be clear from the words, "There is a way that seemeth right unto a man, but the end thereof are the ways of death." [16] The situation ethicist by whatever name throughout the centuries has let loose a flood of behavior flowing out of spiritual degeneracy because there is no absolute standard known, or used if known, to countervail such behavior. Having unleashed such dire consequences of such an ethic, this type person next calls sin good, at least in some situations,[17] and usually with a less than scriptural view of sin.

The situationist religious leader through the ages has approved of sin because he has no personal conviction of the necessity to oppose it. He has approved of sin because he has sought continued acceptance among his fellow men by calling their immorality moral *in the right situation.*

Ezekiel speaks of the horror of this, as he inveighs against false prophets, who "strengthened the hands of the wicked . . . by promising him life." [18]

Moral Standards Needed

Today's cry for freedom is both good and bad, depending on what is meant by it. If the cry for *More* means to get an adequate and decent level of life circumstances and of income, this is justifiable. If by wanting to do what pleases himself a person means that he respects the rights of others as he does so, and at the same time meets the requirements of one's individual roles in life, this is also understandable. True freedom does not permit a constant lust to enjoy life regardless of harmful effects on others and disregard of proper use of one's own person.

Another attitude which is not new and is seen on every side, is that of considering that which is useful to be right merely because it is useful, rather than being right if it is in accord with

God's standards, and wrong if it is not. For example, if self-indulgence of some kind gives temporary enjoyment and is thereby useful to gratify the doer of it, it is wrong if in violation of the Scripture's command against it and all right if the activity is not in such violation. Enjoyment or lack of enjoyment of the pleasure in question is no criterion of right or wrong.

A major principle of law needs careful note today: There never is a time when moral law is not applicable or necessary. Attempts to cut down the Scriptures to the level of folklore and man-made accretions of written matter are not provable. They are also attempts to remove essential structures which God has erected upon which to build man according to His will. Carl F. H. Henry writes in a vein opposite from that of a de-emphasis of biblical morality:

Both in Old Testament and New Testament thought there is but one sure foundation for a lasting civilization, and its cornerstone is a vital knowledge of the redemptive God. In both eras it is wrong to worship false gods, to murder, to commit adultery, and for a reason more ultimate than that the prophet Moses said so. These deeds were wrong before Moses, yea, even before Adam; they have been wrong always, and will be wrong always, because they are antagonistic to the character and will of the Sovereign God of the universe. They are wrong for all creatures anywhere anytime. The universe is put together on moral lines; any attempts to build a civilization on other lines, whether before or after the coming of Jesus Christ into the world, foredooms itself.[19]

Henry's insistence upon moral standards leads us to the word *law*. It is an outgrowth of many factors that law has come in for attack today. The convenient vehicle of those who promote the current fad of the *new morality* is their stirring up of old dialogue about love and law. "All's love, yet all's law," said Wesley, representing the evangelical position succinctly.

The arbitrary uprooting of justice from its inseparable relationship with law has no scriptural ground. Some writers set up an undefined and subjectively experienced love as a rule of life for man, instead of the explicit revelation of God's will in the Scriptures. They say that the gospel is opposite from law, whereas the scriptural concept is that the gospel contains both law and love in order to tell men of their responsibility under God's law and of love's meeting of the demands of God's law in Jesus Christ.

A trend of the day is seen in guidelines by which mob rule is exercised in some instances and by which many people purport to live by a principle of love. Such persons have rejected the standards God proffers without examining them on His terms, or have apostatized from them after partially following them, or have not had them presented to them.

Man's search for *some* standard is visible on every hand. A. Elizabeth Mansfield writes concerning the sex revolution. She quotes several other authorities as concerned that while young people are more sexually permissive, "They are confused and looking for standards by which to govern their sexual behavior, and they need help." [20] Earlier in the same editorial were the significant words, "Young people today believe in a single standard, but with many unresolved questions about what that standard involves." The words about a single standard touch upon two vital factors: Youth in revolt today seem to go *all out* for espousal of one cause, whether that cause be good or not. The hypocritical, complex, many-sided adult is spurned for an adopted cause of one kind or another.

There *is* a single standard, God's Word. There is a cause—the cause of Christ—God's living Word. This is the powerful message we have for youth, the poor, the riotous, for the nonpoor, for all.

References for Chapter 11
1. John 14:6.
2. 1 Corinthians 1:24.

3. Colossians 2:9.
4. 1 Corinthians 2:9.
5. 1 Corinthians 2:14.
6. 1 Corinthians 2:16.
7. Harvey Cox, *The Secular City* (New York, Macmillan Co., 1965), pp. 17, 18.
8. Proverbs 29:18.
9. John 3:3, 5, 7, 8.
10. Arnold M. Rose, *Sociology* (New York, Alfred A. Knopf, 1965), p. 730.
11. William F. Ogburn and Meyer F. Nimkoff, *Sociology* (Boston, Houghton Mifflin Co., 4th ed., 1964), p. 757.
12. Genesis 3:1.
13. Wirt, *Social Conscience*, pp. 91–101.
14. J. Milton Yinger, *Sociology Looks at Religion* (New York, Macmillan Co., 1961), pp. 71, 72.
15. Joseph Fletcher, *Situation Ethics* (Philadelphia, Westminster Press, 1966), p. 153.
16. Proverbs 14:12; 16:25.
17. Isaiah 5:20; Malachi 2:17.
18. Ezekiel 13:22.
19. Carl F. H. Henry, *The Uneasy Conscience of Modern Fundamentalism* (Grand Rapids, Eerdmans, 1947), p. 39.
20. A. Elizabeth Mansfield, "The Sexual Revolution—Its Impact on Child Welfare," *Child Welfare,* Vol. XLVII, No. 7 (July, 1968), p. 380.

12

Cultural Relatives and Absolutes

We have been mentioning subcultures and the larger American culture without discussing cultural factors to any extent, as such. Few subjects are more necessary to understanding today's social action scene.

The Universal Book

The evangelical Christian believes that the Bible is not merely a provincial or sectional book. If it were such, it would be considered under some categories to be only one of the many artifacts associated with a few subcultures of mankind. The advent in the last one hundred years of the study of comparative religions and the development of the classification of man into sociological subgroups have obscured the universality of the Bible. They have made it a handy convenience for the merely nominal Christians to shunt the Bible aside into their convenient discards. It is logical for the nonevangelical to reduce what he calls Christian wisdom to the level of man's wisdom. By these means, humanism and eclecticism attempt many syntheses of biblical and secular philosophies, theologies, and life styles.

Cultural Factors Past and Present

A practical understanding of cultural factors in our nation's past and present will help us understand present-day social action. Cultural relativism and cultural pluralism are terms which somewhat mirror observable sociological facts. Cultural relativism is reflected in the fact that within one culture a given practice is approved, whereas in another the same custom is forbidden. One example of a practice approved by one culture but disapproved by another is polygamy. Another is idol worship. Cultural pluralism is the condition in a society in which several subcultures exist within the main culture, having different customs and group norms from other subcultures and from the main culture. These are allowed to continue side by side as long as they do not interfere with nor violate the laws of the main culture.

Much of the current upheaval in our country today is due to the growth numerically and by influence of cultural diffusion, the sources of which are the American and other blacks, the Mexican-Americans, the American Indians and the Latin Americans. The larger culture, the American whites, receive the effect of this diffusion and return their share.

Economic factors have brought on many crises, but cultural pressures do as well. They stem from deep surges among the minority groups (among majority groups also, it must be realized). These may be recognized to some degree, ranging from slight influence of the mutual assimilation of culture traits through more complete combinations to fusion of two cultures into one.

The evangelical Christian sees all this as a great opportunity. He knows that culture traits in violation of God's moral law will be eliminated as souls seek the Lord in truth.[1] He knows that individuals from a wide variety of subcultures are molded by the Holy Spirit into behavior that is in accordance with the will of God. The challenge in every age is that of lives being changed as God works in human hearts.

Many cultural characteristics do not matter as far as conduct is concerned, and a large latitude of customs and practices may remain stable or change and not violate God's standards either way.[2] On the other hand, we may well ask in the words of Dr. Charles W. Anderson, "Is Christianity moulding our culture or is culture moulding our Christianity?" [3]

Understanding past and present sociocultural factors will help us understand some of the questions confronting our fellow Christians.

Evangelicals in many churches are familiar with the cultural group most dominant in that particular church, and of the community around it (*culture* and *cultural group* here are not to be confused with *refinement* or *social status* or *economic class*). The membership of many churches is mostly or entirely of people of once race, ethnic group, and station in life. In increasing numbers of churches, their memberships are becoming more heterogeneous racially, ethnically, and socially.

Evangelicals United

Along with any one or a combination of the above conditions, there remains within the active evangelical group a divine homogeneity among all believers in the Lord Jesus Christ, in the scriptural sense of the nature of belief. The realization and maintenance of this unity are enjoined more than once in the Bible.[4] Since Jesus was sent to give the "one thing . . . needful," [5] it is logical that His followers concentrate on knowing Him as He wants to be known, and having fellowship with other believers in the unity of the Spirit.

We are faced today with fast-moving developments outside of many of the church doors within which there is an evangelical fellowship. The clamor by surrounding communities that we show our relevance to the present day was formerly almost nonexistent. Now we have an unparalleled opportunity, in the context of the present need, to realize our united position in Christ, to demonstrate it and operate from it as a base.

The secularist says that we have so many diverse people in our nation with divergent beliefs and customs that we can never again be a people of the kind we were at one time with so homogeneous a culture and religious unity. In direct contrast, the evangelical has something specific to say, especially since he is being challenged to justify his position in the community. He can validly say that evangelicals have and always have had a basic ecumenicity in our oneness in Christ, in spite of outward divisions. He can bear witness to the universal bond which unites all believers and to which God invites all men through Christ.

A local church cannot take for granted that it is loved and valued by the community around it. The fact that its witness for Christ is in and of itself of value is not the point. The point is, how can the local church even get to be heard by the few or the many who are within its reach, but who ignore it, tolerate it, or even hate it?

No longer does the Christian go forth into a culture in which that culture expects him to be of the kind of help to it that the Christian wants to be to it. The people in the culture either surmise what we want to give it or are completely ignorant of what we have to give it. (So often we think they know what we want to present, but, almost always, at least in urban areas, they do not know at all.) Whichever the case, they have their own ideas of what they want us to do for them, if they want anything at all. God, responsibility for one's actions so as to give an account to Him, the availability of salvation from Him through the ministry of the church—things which were more or less expected of the church in a bygone day—are not brought to the minds of the people around the church by virtue of that church's presence in the community today, and must be brought to them by active entrance into the community by the church.

In a pluralistic society this is only to be expected, and is symptomatic of the trend away from any degree of theocratic consciousness pervading our society. We do not expect a visible theocracy in this present dispensation. What we can and do have and recommend is the inner rule of God in the lives of His followers, and the extension of that rule as He works in other lives through His witnesses.

The Background of Cultural Pluralism in Our Society

How did it come about that so many cultural elements different from the early American culture have made themselves felt in our society? What are some of the factors in American history which have introduced elements in support of or in opposition to Christian standards into our national life?

Ever since the discovery of the New World, new standards of religion and ethics have entered our country through various peoples from many places on the world's surface. In some sections of our country where the governments in earlier colonial and national days had been very theocratic in nature and in influence, propagation of the gospel was then responsible for a general Christian influence spreading over the young nation. At the same time, dilution of Christian cultural influence has greatly resulted from the entrance of many new and diverse groups of people into our stream of history.

The introduction into our American life of people of various backgrounds causes a new combination of cultural elements among the people. Accompanying racial, ethnic, and religious characteristics are among the main types of influences that cause cultural change. There are alternate strengthening and weakening of norms, ethics, and morals according to the individual characteristics of the people who enter our multicultural agglomeration of peoples.

As a development from out of all this, many Americans do not think of our country as being in any sense a country ruled by God, except in some general sense in which He is a far-distant figure inhabiting the unknown and somehow having some influence over us. This superstitious and sentimental concept is not Christian.

One form of the ignoring of God is that of pouring adverse criticisms on early Americans who magnified God. The Puritans were among such people. The Puritanism and the pietism at which Fletcher scoffs,[6] along with spiritual awakenings and revivals from the earliest days of our country until the present, still have their influence upon our entire culture. It is a sad sight to see that some who profess to be Christians speak in a derogatory way of Puritanism to whom so many of us owe so much. On the other hand, secular writers like Samuel Eliot Morison, after long research, deliberately speak of the constructive and enduring contributions made by the Puritans and go out of their way to refute unjust slurs.[7]

When this writer was a boy in grade school in Philadelphia, he saw evidences of the influences of Puritanism slipping away from community life, even though he did not think of them in that way then. Was it not an evidence of the decline of Puritan effectiveness as well as of Bible influence, when public schools no longer left Wednesday nights free from homework so the children could attend the Wednesday night prayer meeting with the family? When grammar school pupils were told by principals that the singing of hymns and some of the slower music of the past were now better replaced by the jazz music and the dance? When the dress of people then and now became patterned according to the styles set by people without also having an eye to pleasing God? When the central issue was not and is not what music or clothing is right or wrong but *is* deciding to put God first, and then expecting Him to guide the life satisfactorily to Himself and felicitously for His followers?

This is not to say that we should turn back the clock and re-institute vanished customs. Rather it *is* to say that it was the purpose of those customs to assist the individual to worship God. The authorities of the schools assisted in the keeping of pious customs. When they were kept in sincerity they were a means of grace. It is still the Christian's duty to glorify God in all things as the Holy Spirit enables him. This is to be whether or not human authorities assist him in doing so.

In the present day, there is a growing disregard for God's standards as they relate to public morals. For example, there is a clamor from various quarters to brand drunkenness as a private matter rather than a public issue, and to consider adultery as something up to the individuals concerned.

Impact of Cultural Change

Many students of our civilization are alarmed. Our American culture is seen as part of the world culture in which cultural changes of great magnitude are taking place. In the world and in our nation, will the stress of sociocultural change cause collapse of our civilization? This is the concern of George C. Homans, sociologist, versed in world cultures and in cultural anthropology. He writes:

In our view, and here we are following Toynbee again, ancient Egypt and Mesopotamia were civilizations. So were classical India and China: so was the Greco-Roman civilization, and so is our own Western civilization that grew out of medieval Christendom. These societies on the grand scale have had many characteristics in common. At its height, each has been inventive. It has devised and used a more powerful technology than any at the command of the tribes coming before and after it . . . . And almost every one of the civilizations has worked out and adopted a single body of values and beliefs, shared in some degree by all the citizens. Such until recently was Christianity for the Western world . . . .

The appalling fact is that, after flourishing for a span of time, every civilization but one has collapsed. The ruling class, if there was one, has lost its capacity to lead; the formal organizations that articulated the whole have fallen to pieces; the faith has no longer commanded the allegiance of the citizens; much of the technology has even been forgotten for lack of the large-scale cooperation that could put it in effect; and after a last and inevitably futile effort to hold society together by force, the civilization has slowly sunk back to a Dark Age, much like the one from which it started out on its upward path.

The one civilization that has not entirely gone to pieces is our own Western civilization, and we are desperately anxious about it. Can it get out of the rut into which others have fallen? [8]

From the standpoint of some of the verities of Scripture we could take issue with Mr. Homans about how this civilization is next to be visited with drastic transition, and about the extent to which the present civilization has been truly Christian. Our point is made if we note the concern of our fellow Americans for our people. Dare we have less? In the meantime our function is to understand our American society and culture and minister to the people the gospel of God.

A leading economist evaluates our culture as Dr. Richard Hofstadter writes:

Today we have passed out of the economic framework in which that ethic was formed. We demand leisure; we demand that we be spared economic suffering; we build up an important business, advertising, whose function it is to encourage people to spend rather than save; we devise institutional arrangements like installment buying to permit people to spend what they have not yet earned; and we take up an economic theory like that of Keynes which stresses in a new way the economic importance of spending. We think of the economic order in terms of welfare and abundance rather than scarcity; we concern ourselves more with organization and efficiency than with character and punishment and rewards. One of the keys to the controversy of our time over the merits or defects of the "welfare state" is the fact that the very idea affronts the traditions of a great many men and women who were raised, if not upon the specific tenets of social Darwinism, at least upon the moral imperatives that it expressed. The growing divorcement of the economic process from considerations that can be used to discipline human character, and, still worse, our increasing philosophical and practical acceptance of that divorcement, is a source of real torment to the stern minority among us for whom the older economic ethic still has a great deal of meaning. And anyone who today imagines that he is altogether out of sympathy with that ethic should ask himself whether he has never, in contemplating the possibility of a nearly workless economic order, powered by atomic energy and managed by automation, had at least a moment of misgiving about the fate of man in a society bereft of the moral discipline of work.[9]

How many of the changes in our society are fundamental or peripheral, significant or incidental? How men spend their leisure, how they depend on welfare, how they work or prefer not to work under some circumstances are not necessarily evils in themselves. The evil is in covetousness and abuses in all these areas, and in putting self before God and those in need.

Installment buying, deficit spending, use of atomic energy, and automation are with us. Christians have had to make adjustments in their thinking to meet requirements of a kind which would have been outlawed in a Christian economy if they had ever been adopted to begin with. One Christian said in 1933 that a Christian should not have insurance of any kind. Beginning with Social Security and continuing with several other legally and personally required insurances since, he has both had to and wanted to have insurance. And what shall we say about borrowing, charging, or paying interest, and much more?

The whole element of the speed of events and the speed of developments in many fields is one factor that keeps all the world, including Christians, hard pressed to keep up with the dizzy pace. Here, indeed, the Christian does well to be aware of his eternal moorings upon God our Rock. I remember a college professor telling his students that man would soon succeed in splitting the atom. So soon—it happened! Some of the underlying causes of our present confusion have been triggered by the psychology of the atomic age—by the widespread resurgence of the philosophy of "eat, drink and be merry for tomorrow we die" in the face of imminent destruction—and a forsaking of God's standards has ensued. At any rate, a major form this trend is taking is that many people are seeking, sometimes with a passion, to be different; they do not have concern about being right or wrong, they merely strive to be different. How far we will go in dressing dissimilarly (or similarly) or in combining or separating political alignments or in accepting or rejecting social customs, and much more, no one knows. The people of God must learn to live with and be in tune with cultural change and with social change. This is more imperative than ever because of the sharp increase of human need.

Harvey Cox has a pertinent passage:

Scientific technology and medical research have ushered us precipatately into a civilization for which neither our political nor our cultural institutions are prepared. Though our predicament can be partially illuminated by Marx's diagnosis of the economic structure outrunning the political superstructure, in reality our dilemma is a vastly more complex one. We are entering an era in which power is based not on property but on technical knowledge and intellectual skills. We are rushing headlong from the production line to the linear computer, from work to leisure values, from an industrial to an automated society —and our political processes as well as our cultural and religious symbols still reflect the by-gone pre-technical society. Our infant republic has sprouted and shot up in every direction and we can no longer button its clothes around it. We are still trying to dress a fast-growing technological society in political rompers. This lag should have provided us with the catalytic gap we need, but so far it has not. Our accumulating crisis in mass transit, housing, and growing unemployment dramatize our inability to deal politically with the problems created by technological change.[10]

The great strength of evangelical Christianity is that it is not a *dated* religion for the pretechnological era. It is God's vehicle for presenting to the world His eternal salvation for all people everywhere and for all time. The necessity in each generation is not that the salvation be updated, but that the current group of Christians be geared to the age in which they live and skilled in methods to minister to it.

Return to Normalcy

The type culture in which we find ourselves is providing a kind of *natural habitat* in which the Christian can regard himself as living *in* the world while not partaking of the evil behavior of some people in it. Let us see how, in a sense, *return to normalcy* might be a term to describe the present situation of evangelical Christians in the present world.

The facts of history tell us that in a few instances only there have been extended periods of above average outward serenity, morality, and public order. Certainly in the early years of our republic, the Christian influence was potent in education, politics, and society in general. The predominance of truly evangelical Christian denominations made for a much more homogeneous religious picture with outward concomitant results. In contrast to that, it must be remembered that most of the days of Christian history have been testing times for the evangelicals within the Church visible, even in days when the control of Western lands was in the hands of nominal Christianity. The evangelicals, therefore, had little control over the majority of men.

We must note the important distinction that the evangelical Church since its inception has had much *influence* even when it has not had much outward *control*. Because of so much influence which God helped the Church to have, our American past has been replete with many instances in which Christian influences have become Christian control.

Because of the strong early influence of the Church in America, we have been too long accustomed to thinking *we* are the rightful Americans and others of different religions and other backgrounds are usurpers when they gain prominence or control in any sphere of American life. While we are inheritors of a great American evangelical past from the days when Christian influences were of more of a controlling nature than today, we are no less importantly placed than they who served then. The spiritual, social, and cultural characteristics of our surroundings herald for us a more normal *Christian in the world* experience similar to that of most Christians through the ages.

There is much talk these days about our living in a post-Christian era. In some ways this is so very evident, in the light of our trend of thought above. This is one way to speak of our experience as long as it does not imply a kind of defeatism.

Would it not be appropriate in one sense to speak of this as a pre-Christian era? Those of us who believe there will be a physical second coming of Christ to this earth to set up an earthly rule can easily envisage this! [11]

References for Chapter 12

1. Isaiah 55:6, 7.
2. David O. Moberg, *Inasmuch: Christian Social Responsibility in the Twentieth Century* (Grand Rapids, Wm. B. Eerdmans, 1965), pp. 22, 23.

3. Charles W. Anderson, address, 25th Annual Conservative Baptist Meetings (Chicago, Illinois, May, 1968).

4. 1 Corinthians 1:10 et al.

5. Luke 10:42.

6. Fletcher, *Situation Ethics,* pp. 20, 160, 161.

7. Samuel Morison, *The Oxford History of the American People* (New York, Oxford University Press, 1965), pp. 61–74.

8. George C. Homans, *The Human Group* (Harcourt, Brace and Co., 1950), pp. 455, 456.

9. Richard Hofstadter, *Social Darwinism in American Thought* (Boston, The Beacon Press, revised, 1955), p. 40.

10. Cox, *Secular City,* p. 115.

11. 2 Peter 3:13.

13

God and Social Action

Social Welfare Beginnings

Methods of helping people in need have been improved continually, especially in the last one hundred years. However, the history of man helping his fellow man in need is much older than recent history. It is as old as man himself. As part of His common grace, God has put the desire of one person to help another in the human heart, or at least in a very large proportion of human hearts.

The concern of God for His creatures in more than His regular providences is seen strikingly in His provision for His people and for all mankind as when He placed Joseph in the position of administrator under Pharaoh in Egypt during sustained famine. God's miraculous care of His people in their journey to the Promised Land and His continued care of His own in all generations hardly needs mention to those who know His care. The placing of Daniel as administrator during the majority of the seventy years' captivity of the Jews is only one of the many instances of His special care in guiding His chosen people under adverse conditions. Indeed, while we know He exercises constant providential care over all His creatures, it is using the greatest illustration in history to refer to the miraculous preservation of the Jews beginning with the call of Abraham.

God's Provision for Man's Well-Being

God's giving of the Ten Commandments was for the benefit of all mankind. He codified laws which He had promulgated before Sinai and which are binding upon all men forever. They constitute also one major part of the God-revealed standard—the Bible. They constitute also the skeleton of the full law, the fullest manifestation of which is in Christ.[1] The dietary laws of the Pentateuch, the sanitary laws, the agrarian and the ceremonial laws, the city of refuge stipulations—these are climaxed by many precepts about the relationships of the people with one another, with strangers, and with neighboring lands. Throughout these there is evidenced a stress upon care of the poor,[2] the handicapped, the sick, the aging,[3] the bereaved,[4] the abused. Judgment and punishment are specified for oppressors of the people and violators of the law.[5] High within the orbit of the law's coverage are regulations of the family and of family relationships.

Within the whole purview of the law of God, all questions having to do with group relationships are subject to that law as well as are all matters having to do with the behavior of individuals.

In the latter parts of the Old Testament, while not neglected in the Pentateuch, the subject of mistreatment of the poor is prominently treated.[6] At the same time that God thunders against abusing the poor, God also does not condone willful idleness, delinquency, and drunkenness.[7]

New Testament

The New Testament duplicates and adds to the Old Testament pronouncements.[8] Jesus advocated care of the helpless, especially in His account of the Good Samaritan.[9] The early Church set up its own procedures for helping one another in the daily life of the first Christian community at Jerusalem and for ministering to those in need.[10] Further specifications are set forth in the New Testament for doing this, particularly by Paul. There are a few particularly pointed passages in both Old and New Testaments which enjoin helping others. (What is this basically other than social welfare action?) In the midst of hundreds of passages which might be submitted for the purpose, the following seem to be a few which sum up the helping ministry clearly and concisely:

Withhold not good from them to whom it is due, when it is in the power of thine hand to do it. Say not unto thy neighbour, Go, and come again, and tomorrow I will give; when thou hast it by thee.[11]

James reasons identically in his epistle:

If a brother or sister be naked, and destitute of daily food,
And one of you say unto them, Depart in peace, be ye warmed and filled; notwithstanding ye give them not those things which are needful to the body; what doth it profit?
Even so faith, if it hath not works, is dead, being alone.
Yea, a man may say, Thou hast faith, and I have works: shew me thy faith without thy works, and I will shew thee my faith by my works.[12]

Both Solomon and James in these two passages were writing on the basis of God's admonitions to the Israelites to care for their own people. This would also include the "strangers within their gates." If under the law it was the expected thing to help all comers in need when possible to do so, certainly under grace the Christian obligation is to do at least that much. In the next passage quoted, the same inclusion of people outside the congregation of believers is very clear:

"As we have therefore opportunity, let us do good unto all

men, especially unto them who are of the household of faith." [13]

Also, Jesus as the Prime Doer of good sets up an example for Christians to follow: ". . . God anointed Jesus of Nazareth with the Holy Ghost and with power: who went about doing good, and healing all that were oppressed of the devil; for God was with him." [14]

The Apostle John, in characteristic concern for the love of God in our hearts, says: "Hereby perceive we the love of God, because he laid down his life for us: and we ought to lay down our lives for the brethren. But whoso hath this world's good, and seeth his brother have need, and shutteth up . . . his compassion from him, how dwelleth the love of God in him?" [15]

There is a great passage in Matthew which speaks of deeds of individuals as they relate to judgment. While it is a specific pronouncement in connection with a special situation in Jesus' day and another event in the prophetic future, the whole truth of the caring for or the not caring for the needs of our fellow men and the results of each policy can be seen in the vivid passage. Matthew does not need to bring into his writing the express stipulations of the Old Testament that each follower of God is to help the helpless. He *begins* with them as an understood base and goes on to speak incisively about future events of judgment.

Key parts of this passage are: "Inasmuch as . . . ye have done it unto me . . . . Inasmuch as ye did it not to one of the least of these, ye did it not to me. And these shall go away into everlasting punishment: but the righteous into life eternal." [16]

Revivals and Awakenings [17]

In Bible days and since, God has sent outpourings of His grace in what have been called *revivals*. The word revival is appropriate when God revives what has already begun, i.e., the life of Christ in the believer or a group of individual believers.

When it is a reference to the conversion of those who have not yet become Christians and are therefore in the death and darkness of sin, the term should be *spiritual awakening*. For convenience sake the term revival is often used for both types of experience.

When revivals and spiritual awakenings occur, as one would expect, the spiritual lives of those affected are greatly influenced. Invariably, great personal and social problems in their lives are also affected.

God's action is truly social action, insofar as the interaction of His messengers with their hearers results in wide social change. So many people are changed that they in turn influence the people and circumstances in their environments. The social institutions of the family, the government, the economic life and more are greatly affected, with long-lasting results.

Bible Revivals

A study of *Bible revivals* in the Kingdom of Judah shows that much more than flurries of poor relief, political reform, and ceremonial fidelity resulted therefrom. The revivals seemed to show results especially in one or another sector of social life, while the other areas were also affected. The revival under Asa brought about religious reforms at a time when the young nation needed to be directed to seek the Lord.[18] Under Jehoshaphat, education of the people in the godly life notably resulted.[19] The Jehoiada-Joash renewal emphasized God's primacy in the political life.[20] Wide-sweeping changes under Hezekiah resulted in focus on personal sanctification with restorations of national spiritual objectives.[21] Under the most exemplary Josiah, national obedience to God was highlighted with results in many areas of social relationships.[22]

Under Nehemiah, revival produced political, religious, and social improvement.[23] The quality of revival mentioned as occurring under Zerubbabel [24] and recommended under Ezekiel [25] was shed upon the new young Christian at Pentecost and thereafter.[26]

Revivals in America

We realize that revival may be local or widespread, lasting for shorter or longer times. They may affect few or many areas of human experience. They also may pervade entire cultures and nations for a very long time. It is too easy for students of history to assign events to their proper chronological periods and assume that such events were of the kind which would not occur again in that way. This type of interpretation stems from an evolutionary outlook on history which presupposes an event like a spiritual awakening would not happen again, or at least not show the same outward characteristics. It is their loss, because they fail to see such things happening even when they might be living in the midst of such events.

We believe with Timothy L. Smith that, "Revivalistic religion and the quest of Christian perfection lay at the fountainhead of our nation's heritage of hope." [27] We hold also that this is still true and that true revival and spiritual awakening are phenomena which may occur now should God choose to bring them about.

Early American revivals like those under Jonathan Edwards and George Whitefield exerted great influence for righteousness in their day and long afterward. Awakenings under Charles G. Finney and Dwight L. Moody are still bearing fruit in many parts of this country and abroad. Nor is this to be said to be confined only to former days. Results of revivals and spiritual awakenings, sometimes spreading over large areas of the world, can be identified as resulting from the ministries of Billy Sunday, Billy Graham, and a host of present-day evangelists in this country and abroad.

True revivals are not merely spiritual excursions but powerful causes of social and cultural change. Specific social action of a beneficial kind follows, as souls stirred by God's power produce good social acts.

Some Revival Results

Not only does true revival give birth to beneficial social action, but it also produces men who are intensely involved in yet more such social action. As we look back over history we see that great revival produces men who were greatly involved in specific projects to benefit mankind, both spiritually and physically. The great Jonathan Edwards was interested in battling disease, so much so that he died early because he gave himself to be used as a volunteer in testing a smallpox vaccine. John Wesley set up clinics in London to give medical help to the poor. George White-field had his orphanage interests.

Many of the English "Clapham Sect" took a hand in social reform. William Wilberforce of antislavery fame was an evangelical, a great social action catalyst. Robert Raikes, founder of Sunday Schools, gathered his Gloucester boys for his *ragged schools*. Charles Finney with his attacks on social ills, the Seventh Earl of Shaftesbury with opposition to child labor, and Dwight L. Moody with his concern for the city poor, are but a few of the evangelicals who went beyond their preaching ministries to help people in dire need.

Moberg says: "Evangelical Christianity was a major influence in many social reforms in industrial societies during the eighteenth and nineteenth centuries. It had a profound impact upon the abolition movement, prison reform, the treatment of the mentally ill, and working conditions of industrial laborers in England (factory reform). The concern of evangelicals for human needs led to the establishment of many welfare societies which helped to alleviate the effects of social ills. Much zealous concern for social welfare can be traced to the compassion originally awakened by revivalists for sinning and suffering men." [28]

There is no desire on the part of evangelicals to say that only evangelicals have brought about social action and consequent reform. It is our contention that God works through any men he chooses to bring about improvement in society by the operation of His common grace.

Until the advent of the *social gospel* in the last third of the nineteenth century, there was little differentiation made in modern times between spiritual and social reform beyond the separation some interpreters always make between them. Since the advent of the social gospel, evangelicals have been blamed for retreating from the arena of social concern and action. We shall see to what extent this is so and not so. Since beneficial social change results from the operation of spiritual power, does this mean that evangelicals do not have spiritual power since social action is not one of their strengths (or is *said* not to be one of their strengths) today?

It is the opinion of some evangelicals who have observed such trends for many years that in some areas of action the evangelicals have always done better than any other group and are still excelling. These observers believe that evangelicals will always excel when they know all the facts in each case and are shown what and where to do what is needed and how to accomplish the task.

References for Chapter 13
1. Matthew 5:17.
2. Leviticus 25:35; Deuteronomy 15:7; Proverbs 19:17.
3. Leviticus 19:32.
4. Exodus 22:22; Isaiah 1:17.
5. Ezra 7:26; Ecclesiastes 8:11.
6. Amos 2:6; Isaiah 3:15.

7. Proverbs 6:6–11; 21:17; 23:21.
8. Galatians 2:10; James 1:27; 1 Timothy 5:1.
9. Luke 10:30–37.
10. Acts, chapters 2–6, et al.
11. Proverbs 3:27, 28.
12. James 2:15–18.
13. Galatians 6:10.
14. Acts 10:38.
15. 1 John 3:16, 17.
16. Matthew 25:34–46.
17. The author's studies in revivals and spiritual awakenings were greatly aided by the teaching of Dr. Albert G. Johnson, pastor emeritus of Hinson Memorial Baptist Church, Portland, Oregon, to whom the indebtedness is here expressed. His influence is seen in this particular part of the text.
18. 2 Chronicles 15:2–15.
19. 2 Chronicles 17:1–10.
20. 2 Chronicles 23:16–21; 24:1.
21. 2 Chronicles 29:3–36; 30:1–26.
22. 2 Chronicles 34:3–33; 35:1–19.
23. Nehemiah, especially chapters 8, 9, 10.
24. Zechariah 4:6, 10.
25. Ezekiel 36:26.
26. Joel 2:28–32; Acts, chapter 2.
27. Timothy L. Smith, *Revivalism and Social Reform* (New York, Abingdon Press, 1951), p. 7.
28. Moberg, *Christian Social Responsibility*, p. 17.

14

Social Implications of the Gospel

Social Awareness

Evangelical Christians have been alternately very conscious of social issues and very unaware of them. At times, they have been aware of social needs but not able to do anything about them. This was often because of being prohibited from doing anything. Sometimes they did not have facilities with which to operate. There was often not a favorable climate of public opinion within which to labor. Sometimes in the past, evangelicals have been in a position to lead effective action against social evils, as when they have been in power in state churches in Europe, or in theocratic type communities in America. Sometimes they have been dissenting minorities in strong opposition to majority practice. Our reason for taking a look at the social implications of the gospel is twofold: There is some climate of evangelical willingness at this very time to listen to any plausible suggestions for social action against social ills. There is also an awakening conviction on the part of evangelicals that action must be taken to carry out the suggestions.

Within the last one hundred years there have been very noticeable divorcements between the view some evangelicals have had on matters of faith and spiritual life, and the view they have had on the works of righteousness they are to do in the world around them. Prior to that time, there had been no major separation of the one sphere from the other except in evangelical sects in which such a separation had been a regular characteristic of those sects all along. These particular evangelicals last referred to had sincere doctrinal convictions that they were pleasing God by emphasizing their difference from the lives of those outside their midst by isolating themselves from them. In some such instances, they felt they were merely different from others. In other instances, they not only felt *different from,* but *superior to,* other people. These are still the earmarks of some Christians today.

As sin has increased in quantity and complexity, the number among evangelicals who have deliberately cultivated a separation from the world has increased. (By separation from the world in this context we are thinking of isolation from the people in the world and their needs, and not that separation from the world which is commanded in the sense of avoiding compromise with sinners in their sin.[1]) On the one hand, evangelicals who have thus separated themselves have given new strength to the former group who sincerely stood against spiritual corruption for scriptural reasons. On the other hand, there have been and there still are others who use the Scriptures as an occasion to justify a kind of monastic retreat from reality. This is perhaps an admission that they have not let the Lord Jesus Christ give them victory in Himself without attempting to flee the world. They should take a stand and trust Him for victory.[2] Only the Lord knows what motive each Christian has that would cause him to oppose the evils of this world in this kind of escape instead of standing for the Lord in His strength without retreating.

We know we are not to love the world of lust and of concentration on the pride of life and material possessions.[3] Yet we are to love our neighbors as ourselves, which, along with loving

God, is the essence of the law and the prophets.[4] The times that are upon us demand that we hold to that proper doctrinal base and godly limit which we ought to maintain in conducting our lives in a needy world,[5] but also seek how we may go the second mile [6] to help the spiritually and materially destitute of our generation.

There is another and many-sided factor dating from about 1865 which explains why many evangelicals retreated into isolation from social involvement. As it became more clear that the American culture was becoming pluralistic and not more but less subservient to the Scripture standard of faith and life, a frequent first reaction was to retreat in defense and keep the nucleus pure and safe from contamination. There was also the refusal of the evangelical to identify himself with theologically liberal programs of good works which did not insist upon the centrality of the Bible and of Jesus as God's eternal Son and the only Saviour of men.

"This aversion against combining with liberal-sponsored programs gave rise to reactions against the social programs of the modern reformers. This grew in part . . . out of the conviction that desirable ends were being sought in an undesirable or ineffective context . . . world peace, the brotherhood of man, democracy, and the new economy hardly meant for religious liberalism and humanism what they meant for evangelicalism; . . . its ends, as well as its methods, were distinct from the non-evangelical movements. The non-evangelicals were striving for *inadequate ends*." [7]

What Dr. Henry means by *inadequate ends* he explains by pointing out that true world peace could not have been a possible achievement without having a scriptural view of the Person and work of Christ in mind and an awareness that only He could bring it about, by biblically prescribed means and ends. Henry goes on to note that it was felt that it was useless to oppose the liquor traffic or to deal with problems of labor and management directly without first getting the hearts of men guilty of evil to change as God works in them by His Spirit.[8]

The Social Gospel

There have been and are many theoreticians who focus on the group rather than the individual as the key object for setting up and carrying out social action strategy. They deem the group greater than the individual, thinking of the group as greater than the sum of its parts.

Social gospel advocates leaned in that direction. "But sin is more than individual; it is transmitted socially through custom." [9] Even when the social gospel was spoken of in relation to the individual, the individual is seen only as a unit that affects and is affected beneficially by the improving world around him: "The saved life must function socially or be lost . . . Once let this gospel message of the worth of a man in terms of his possible Christlikeness get possession of the world and social regeneration will follow." [10] In this, the error is not only in what is said but also very much in what is not said. Mathews does not identify the saved life as one both now and eternally redeemed from sin, cleansed by the blood of Christ.

It is worth noting here that today, many sincere and some not so sincere advocates of social action are so enamored of manipulating groups of people to bring about change that they even specify that the day of the individual is past. Jesus always put individual souls first in His ministry on earth, whether in sermons to multitudes or in personal interviews. This matter of the individual and the group figures in a further way in a later chapter, but here as we scan the social gospel we especially note that the entire Scriptures focus on the individual: "The soul that sinneth" [11]—he that believeth . . . ." [12]

Man, as viewed by advocates of the social gospel, is basically good. Therefore his *Christlikeness* is something which is said to grow from his inner goodness into a social regeneration of society as other members of society improve similarly by his influence. Christ is not seen as more than a man. The Holy Spirit is not God and His Name is merely a euphemistic term for the influence of God. "The idea of Jesus embodied in the church will spread throughout society; the Spirit of God in Christianity can work to the regeneration of a world of cruelty and selfishness and sin, both individually and socially." [13]

It is frustrating to the evangelical to see words like *sin* and *regeneration* used, when he knows that the liberals mean very different things by them than he does. For instance, regeneration is thought of by the liberal as reformation by man's good intentions and good works rather than through transformation by God the Holy Spirit.

This social gospel, with its belief in the innate goodness of man, is at the very outset opposed to the evangelical view that man is a depraved sinner, incapable of regenerating himself or society. Henry says: "Evangelicalism saw in such moralistic movements the subtle proclamation of a higher, respectable way of life that stood nevertheless at a far remove from the redemptive regeneration of the New Testament, which the church was commissioned to proclaim to the nations. The moralism of pagan idealism was being substituted for the biblical 'good news.' " [14]

Evangelicals today have so often seen Jesus presented as a mere man, such as in institutions of learning or by communications media. He is represented as merely one of the several great religious leaders of the world without His being designated as the Son of God and God Incarnate. We who are used to knowing Christ personally believe in Him as the Scriptures present Him. We do not often think of the many people who never have Christ presented to them in any other way than as a mere man. For their sakes, and for those who have not heard of Him at all, evangelicals should of all people be among the first to minister to the basic needs of our fellow men. Such ministrations can then be used by the Holy Spirit to open the door to the hearts of those assisted. A presentation of the Lord Jesus Christ as He truly is can then follow.

Evangelical Resumption of Social Responsibility

It is hard to see how there can be a relationship between former efforts to *bring the kingdom in* by good deeds and today's action ranging from deeds of mercy to those of violent destruction.

Deviousness of the human heart, however, will lead men to any action of any kind, violent or serene, as long as it offers a substitute for God's prescribed behavior for men.

In the light of such extreme manifestations of spiritual bankruptcy in the Church at large, the evangelicals should wake to the clarion call of a mandate from God to reenter the lists of Christian social action. In a sense the evangelicals are being brought back to where they left off. They withdrew from collaboration with heterodox theologians and most of their followers in social reform movements. Because they had objected to unorthodox doctrine, they were in turn ostracized and made unwelcome, ridiculed as obscurantists.

Since World War II, as a result of which man's innate goodness was called in question and thought by some to be a fictitious idea (not to be confused with man's inestimable worth and potential), evangelicals have been listened to more. There is truth to this statement at least in circles in which there is impartial acceptance of their efforts to work with community leaders in endeavors where there is no doctrinal compromise involved. After all, theologies keep coming and going, but the revelation of God in Christ is constant. As evangelicals adhere to that, they come to represent something which is unchanging.

Evangelicals do not believe in the social gospel as it is so called because they do not believe the gospel needs the prefix of the word *social* before it. The gospel itself is an instrument used in social interaction and has powerful effects in both problematic and normal social situations. They *do* believe that the *true* gospel is the message about a Saviour who transforms lives, and that as a result the transformed person produces works which flow out from the changed life. Good social action starts with the individual Christian and his influence in the world.

Evangelist Graham sums it up for evangelicals: "I lay a great deal of emphasis on the social applications of the Gospel. For a Christian to ignore the social problems around him is a tragedy . . . my first responsibility is to win men to Christ; then and only then can and will they live as Christians in the world." [15]

True, evangelicals did withdraw too much in the past from their social responsibilities. Also in the past, there were, and today are, many more exceptions to that statement than are generally realized. Now, with the social problems explosion that is upon us, it is going to take some doing indeed for anyone to stay completely removed from the needs of society. Nor does an evangelical really want to shirk. When evangelicals are aroused, convinced, informed, and led, there is little likelihood of their not helping.

References for Chapter 14
1. 2 Corinthians 6:14–18.
2. Moberg, *Christian Social Responsibility*, p. 20.
3. 1 John 2:15–17.

4. Matthew 22:37–40; Leviticus 19:18.
5. Titus 2:12.
6. Matthew 5:41.
7. Henry, *Uneasy Conscience,* p. 30.
8. *Ibid.,* pp. 31, 32.
9. Charles H. Hopkins, *The Rise of the Social Gospel in American Protestantism* (New Haven, Yale University Press, 1940), p. 231.
10. Shailer Mathews, *The Social Gospel* (Philadelphia, The Griffith and Rowland Press, 1910), pp. 15, 16.
11. Ezekiel 18:4.
12. John 3:16, 36, et al.
13. Mathews, *op. cit.,* p. 30.
14. Henry, *Uneasy Conscience,* p. 32.
15. Billy Graham, "My Answer," St. Paul *Dispatch* (July 23, 1964), p. 20 in Moberg, *op. cit.,* p. 16.

15

Christians and the Development of Social Welfare

Social Welfare in Historical Perspective

We now direct our attention to social welfare developments outside the Church, in order to describe the Church's part in them and thereby give some perspective for understanding the part the Church has had in social welfare action.[1] In fact, the development of social welfare services and of the social work profession as they are today were greatly influenced by evangelical Christians through the years.

It is customary to say that welfare services as we know them today in America were especially occasioned by the increase of population, including major increases by immigration. It is also known that living and working conditions caused by the Industrial Revolution and by urbanization added more welfare needs. It is not usually remembered that the pattern of American social welfare services were partly set up in the early days of the colonists because they had the Elizabethan Poor Laws of 1601 to use as a model in devising American poor relief. When the young nation experienced waves of immigration and the accompanying factors of industrialization and urbanization combined to cause multiplying welfare needs, social welfare services were devised in addition to the basic legal and charitable efforts to ameliorate human need.

The account of the development of social welfare services in the United States is in part a chronicle of the development of the social work profession in response to social welfare needs.

Social welfare as a specific kind of provision of social service to people is thought of as developing only in the last few centuries. Yet, social welfare is as old as man. Social welfare organization on its modern scale has been comparatively recent and has had to become a complex operation to deal with the more complex problems of our day. There are many places and situations in which the basic idea of social welfare is reflected. One person helps another because for some reason he cannot bear to see him be neglected. Another person helps a person in need because it is a custom of society to help the helpless. Whatever the motive, most people have been willing to help their fellows in time of need, or at least to think that they *ought* to be helped. Social welfare, then, is provision by people so that their neighbors in need might have their help to fare well (hence, welfare).

Among the declared purposes of the founding of these United States of America is to "promote the general Welfare, and secure the Blessings of Liberty to ourselves and to our Posterity." [2] Much discussion has taken place over whether or not the phrase *the general welfare* can be thought to refer to social welfare. It certainly is much more than the restricted use of *social welfare* as we use it today, but there is no reason to believe that it did not include some of this thought.

Not to be forgotten today is the phrase "Blessings of Liberty." By constitutional amendment and other legislation United States citizens are free. Many of them, however, are without some of the simplest blessings of freedom. Many disadvantaged citizens in rural pockets of poverty and urban ghettos are not sure that the voices of concern for them are sincere voices. Both the needed material assistance and the right attitude of understanding and giving are the most vital ingredients in any gesture which might be extended to those who are without some of the blessings of freedom.

Families usually assume responsibility for helping to meet emergency needs of their own family members. Yet, today, due to the smaller number of extended families, some individual families who have no grandparents, siblings, aunts, uncles, cousins to look to in time of need are obliged to turn to community welfare facilities for help. Even when there are extended family connections for some to use in ordinary times, those same connections cannot help now due to the inroads of poverty in their midst.

Such demands as these have materially increased the originally small number of dependent persons calling for community help, since colonial days. As community resources gradually became thus increased and funds were limited, it occurred to the local community leaders in the middle and late nineteenth century that part-time welfare workers were not sufficient provision of personnel to handle welfare operations.

This need for more personnel was first felt in large cities. This does not mean that there were not previously many county workers in rural areas when more of our population was agrarian. It means that the need to specialize in doing social welfare visitation as an occupation and for wages became evident in city settings. They were like many such workers today who are full-time workers in welfare services without having professional training for their work. They may have had then, as now, on-the-job training for their work as social welfare operations became better organized.

Social Work Professionalization

Eventually the term *social worker*, first used in America about 1861, became the way of referring to full-time workers in the social services. By the end of the nineteenth century, formal education for full-time social workers was begun. This was in the form of the first graduate schools of social work which grew out of more informal educational programs beginning a generation earlier. By 1915, the social work profession was more fully envisioned and began to take shape. By 1955, the formation of the National Association of Social Workers signalled that a formal structure of a new helping profession had been matured and consolidated to take its place alongside medicine, law, nursing, teaching, and the profession that had been first in point of time in the helping professions, the ministry.

We have previously seen how communities plan ways to meet social needs as these needs are uncovered in the occurrence of social problems. They set up goals to reach in dealing with the problems, and formulate a social policy which guides their procedure. The climax comes in the social action taken to carry out the social policy. Varieties of social action used within the framework of community organization are of interest at this point in our study, because these are a large segment of the social action output today. They have long been such, because social welfare departments and other social agencies have always been the places from which social workers have originated services for those in need.

When abnormal behavior of individuals or groups causes special action, such special action is conscious, planned action, taking the form of specific sanctions or more elaborate programs of correction, prevention, and cure. "Social action rests on the activities of all citizens using techniques of public education and propaganda, social legislation, and cooperative and collective enterprises." [3]

Another related use of *social action* is made by social workers: "When the social worker turns to the forces of community and government to achieve his objectives . . . this process is thought of as 'social action.' " [4]

Elimination of problems and the alleviation of human suffering, along with attempts at prevention of recurrence of these factors, are the goal of professional social work efforts. "The term 'social action' as used in social work, describes activities of social work organizations at agencies that are directed toward achieving a better adaptation of social policy and social institutions to the actual needs of people as observed in social work practice." [5]

Social action is described in the *Encyclopedia of Social Work* as the term commonly applied to an aspect of organized social welfare activity which attempts to close the gap between normal social functioning of individuals in a normal society and the inadequate social functioning of individuals who are beset with social needs and problems. Elizabeth Wickenden, who writes in that vein, goes on to point out that there are times when "the social action aspect of social welfare tends to be obscured by the daily exigencies of the job at hand." [6] Today, however, there is evidence that social workers are more primarily social action conscious than at any time in thirty years.

The Church and Other Nongovernment Helping Organizations Aid Government Agencies

In the seventeenth, eighteenth and nineteenth centuries, and even up to Depression times in the twentieth century in our country, governmental social welfare relief was deemed no more than hardly enough to meet most community welfare needs. Local relief help was not usually sought unless family resources and the assistance of neighbors and friends were exhausted. The able-bodied person was usually able to get work. Social action by social welfare authorities to provide for people in need beyond basic welfare provisions in local law was a last resort, held in reserve when these other sources of aid failed.

Children worked, not too many older people were alive because life expectancy was well under that of fifty years of age, and unemployment was minimal except for occasional emergencies. Before too many handicapped, orphaned, sick, and elderly people overtaxed local facilities, all but the largest cities got by without having to call for help from state governments to too large an extent in the form of more funds and facilities. The growth of needs beyond power of governmental agencies to help developed somewhat as follows:

As demand occurred, supplementary relief to people in need was given by agencies other than those of local government. Church benevolence funds were a major source of help to the needy. Associations of private individuals toward the end of the seventeenth century began to organize the first secular philanthropic organizations, which, along with individual philanthropists, carried much of the burden of relief, augmenting the limited public funds. These private welfare services continue today.

Local relief under town and county auspices was the major source of public welfare help to the needy before the American Civil War. During the first half of the nineteenth century, the first conditions of congestion in large cities brought about the first large-scale social welfare visitation to city tenements among the poor. From the Civil War until the beginning of the twentieth century, state welfare departments were formed to meet increased needs of welfare administration, and took the burden of growing welfare problems.

In the latter half of the nineteenth century, mental hospitals began to develop and social casework grew as a method of social welfare service. Settlement house beginnings and early community organization efforts also came upon the scene as urban congestion and problems multiplied.

From the early days of the twentieth century until the Great Depression, the federal government had to take more and more responsibility for social welfare action because problems had increased even more. Social welfare services advanced contemporarily with movements for women's rights and child labor reform in the early days of the century.

These were followed by developments in the areas of psychiatric social work, medical social work, and the larger use of social group work practice.

The role of the Church, and evangelicals in particular, has been a major one. Religious auspices of all kinds with any facilities at all sought to meet the social challenges of their day. The nineteenth century saw development of missions for canal workers, the beginnings of the YMCA, and of religious work to reach railroaders and inner city dwellers, and the start of city rescue missions. Mounting attacks by reformers upon slum conditions included those which bred bad health. The Salvation Army, begun in England, took up work in this country. Numerous denominational city missions and home missions efforts date from that period.

Evangelical ministries did much to help in a day when the philosophy of the United States government was that local and not national government should be responsible for relief or charity. The views of the evangelicals by and large included expectations that social service would accompany and follow evangelization.

Separation of Church and State

One factor was significant in addition to the foregoing, which has far-reaching implications for later patterns for social welfare policy and action. When Church and State were viewed as so definitely separate, the psychology of the situation more and more relegated care of needy persons already under Church oversight to the care of the Church and all others to the care of the county or the town. Partly because of this, it was from that time, at the end of the eighteenth century, that church workers did not venture to help most people beyond the group for which they were responsible. They considered that those not in their own congregations who were in need were by law relegated to care by governmental units, and that those who were familiar with the church's facilities as parishioners or at least connected with church members in some way were eligible to get help within church precincts.

These tendencies in religious settings have persisted until today. Government agencies are often viewed incorrectly as not willing to work with church-related agencies. On the other hand, churches are not too often thought of as being desirous of collaboration with community welfare programs. Also, churches in those days assumed largely that government, while not church-dominated, was at least a Protestant-controlled segment of our national life. Therefore, there was on the part of the churches no objection to government doing welfare work that was not directly the concern of the churches.

It must be admitted that some church groups by conviction always kept to themselves, aiding their own members and occasionally any others for whom they felt responsible. Other churches which had been active in ministries to the needy on a larger scale succumbed to the prevailing relegation of welfare ministries to government. From a day when (especially in New England) Church and State were closely allied and often governed by the same people, to a day when welfare services are largely secularized, many changes in public social policy have taken place.

References for Chapter 15

1. At many points in Part II, and especially from here to the end, many of the major threads of thought were discussed with Dr. William Culbertson in March 1962 in connection with the theme of evangelism and Christian social service in ministry to America as a mission field. The summary of that conversation written down then by the author is a kind of miniature of Part II of this book in several ways.
2. *Constitution of the United States of America,* preamble.
3. Gordon Hamilton, *Theory and Practice of Social Casework* (New York, Columbia University Press, 1951), p. 14.
4. *Idem.*
5. National Association of Social Workers, *Goals, op. cit.,* p. 7.
6. Elizabeth Wickenden, "Social Action," *Encyclopedia of Social Work* (1965), p. 698.

16

Religion and Social Work

Religious (Sectarian) Social Work

It is more necessary than ever that persons who help people in need learn how to work with other *helping* people. Social work and the ministry are helping professions as are teaching, medicine, nursing, law.

A few terms need defining and clarification as to their usage. Professional social work usage is indicated here.

Religious social work is done in religious agencies.

Sectarian social work is the same as religious social work. It is a technical term used as part of social work professional jargon. It is used interchangeably with the term religious social work.

The term sectarian social work is used without most of the connotations we place on the word *sect* within evangelical circles. It is social work as distinguished from secular social work, which is any social work done outside religious settings.

When we use religious or sectarian social work as terms we shall mean by them what professional social workers usually mean: It is social work done in any religious setting, such as, Catholic, Jewish, Protestant social service.[1] The evangelical Christian social worker shall usually be referred to in this text by the use of the word *evangelical*.

We must further note a principle which has already caught

182

our attention and which Christianity and Judaism have long espoused. Social work prides itself as a profession which cherishes it as one of its basic tenets. This is the primacy and importance of the individual. While it is true that the group can function in ways and achieve results which the individual alone cannot, the group could not even exist without individuals. In fact, the group situation was made by God for man, so as to meet the needs of the individual.[2]

Social work, in spite of growing out of social welfare developments stemming in large degree from Judaeo-Christian influences, is neither Jewish nor Christian as such. In the broader sense in which it is a manifestation of God's common grace, it is a part of the application of God's wisdom as he enables man to help man. In the dichotomous sense in which man separates between sacred and secular, social work is secular in character and attempts to be as objective as it can be in view of its scientific orientation. It is not, as such, contrary to nor identical with religious teaching or ideology, in spite of contentions that it is antireligious, a-religious, partly religious, or completely religious. It is a *method* used by people regardless of their degree of religiosity.

Social work insists that it is as professionally objective as the medical, legal, or teaching professions. The Christian who is a social worker is able to function just as professionally as a Christian who is a doctor or lawyer or teacher. The professional does the specific piece of work which is called for at the time without interrupting any part of it to talk about spiritual matters.

This does not prevent Christian social workers from inserting Christian content within what is a valid sectarian social work setting. Nor does it prevent the professional from dealing with religious and spiritual matters when and as they normally arise within the professional situation even in a secular setting. This latter view is accepted in professional circles.[3] In the author's opinion, it is unprofessional for any professional social worker to avoid any truly religious factors in individual or group situations as long as the factors are handled properly. To refuse to handle these issues as they arise is damaging, unless the refusal or avoidance is indicated in the best interest of the client at a given point, or the social worker is not equipped to handle them himself. If he is unable for any reason to handle such content properly, he should refer the person in need to someone in the same agency or elsewhere who can do so.

Relations Between Religious Groups and Social Work

Part of the evangelical protest against liberal theology was directed against social work. This was largely because social gospel advocates identified themselves more closely with the emphasis made by social work on doing good to our fellow men, while the evangelicals felt to some degree that secular influences should be avoided.

Such influences were in the form of active antireligious sentiment among some social workers, and in some adverse criticisms of religion by some philosophical and psychological points of view espoused by some social workers. When we say antireligious we do not mean usual stereotypes of rabid and ranting atheistic denunciation of religion. There are those who say there are enough values present in religion that conflict with social work values so that they can never be linked too closely, even though the religious side of man is a reality that must be reckoned with in understanding human personality. References are often made to instances in which *religion* has caused mental and nervous disorder. (Reference is not made in such instances to the millions of cases in which true religion has prevented or cured many disorders.) Also, there are many professional social workers who believe that there is a close identity between many of the values of religion and of social work, so that the differences are admitted where they exist so as to improve efficient service to people in need.

Additional secular influences which the evangelicals thought should be avoided included the close identification of social work with government welfare programs. Some evangelicals became wary of governmental domination of their own agencies and of more and more possible intrusion of big government into religious circles, which would violate the principles of the separation of Church and State.

Some of this feeling stemmed from the onset of the Great Depression in 1929, when the federal government was forced into large-scale involvement in social welfare activity. Pressures upon government in turn caused it to reach out for help to agencies already in existence. Whether or not such a view was justified in all cases, some agencies viewed the government as intrusive and unjustifiably dictatorial. This included some church-related institutions and some rescue missions. Whether or not caused by ignorance of government collaboration with various agencies through the previous years, or by clashes of social and political philosophies with religious factors, the estrangement of some religious groups from any association with secular welfare programs has been especially strong from that time until recently.

There is no doubt that, on the professional social work side, there have been many who believe that religion and social work should not and cannot mix. Some writers representing both sides of the question continue to belabor this subject in controversial writing, as evangelical Professor Alan Gruber is constrained to do.[4] Part of this continuing discussion stems from times when religious and social work agencies opposed one another in times of crisis. The present times of crisis dictate that such residual animosities be scrapped in favor of seeking the maximum of collaboration of parties on both sides.

In line with this necessity, a new trend in the social work profession became noticeable in the last decade or more. In the fields of sociology and psychology, religion has been more and more conceived of as one of the basic social institutions of society, which has favorably conditioned the minds of social work students to look more realistically on the religious element in human experience. Religious assistance in areas dealt with by social work is also being recognized. Herbert Stroup speaks of the rapprochement of religion and social work:

"The growth of social work in the United States cannot be fully understood without constant recourse to the contributions of religious persons and organizations . . . at present there is a strong inter-relationship between religion and social work . . . Many social workers not employed by sectarian agencies cherish religion—as does the citizen generally—and seek to interpret its significance for their lives and professional practice . . . The important question for religion and social work is not the fact of their relationship, but how concretely and in what detail they can and do relate to each other. This problem is pertinent, for example, in a day when social workers are concerned with urgent recruitment programs." [5]

Certainly, although it might appear on the surface that the appalling shortage of social workers now might influence social work to make concessions to religion in order to enlist its help with social problems, this is not a valid assumption. There are more pertinent reasons for renewed relationships. Dean Werner Boehm, Director and Coordinator of the (1959) Curriculum Study produced by the Council on Social Work Education, writes: "It is obvious that social and psychological factors are clearly interrelated with spiritual well-being. Thus it becomes

difficult to determine where social work ends and ministry begins
or where ministry ends and social work and psychiatry begins." [6]
In the same place, Boehm names the ministry along with social
work, education, law, and medicine as one of the major *helping
professions.*

Describing the process that has been taking place in the
relationship of religion to social welfare, Charles G. Chakerian
says: "Religious bodies . . . constitute an integral segment of
the American system of social welfare that today is divided into
three broad categories of programs; those under the sponsorship
of government agencies at the local, state and/or federal levels;
those of voluntary nonsectarian organizations; and those of a
great variety of religious bodies . . . a growing number of
religious bodies are looking for persons who possess both the
bachelor of divinity and master of arts or master of social work
degrees . . . Sponsoring religious bodies are increasingly considering their welfare work to be not something peripheral to
their central tasks but rather an integral part of their total
ministry . . . The place of religion in professional welfare education, theory, and practice is receiving increasing attention . . .
The indications are that they [religiously sponsored social welfare
programs] will continue for a long time to be a significant segment
of American social welfare." [7]

Social Work—the Individual and the Group

We have had occasion to discuss the importance of the individual to God and to the evangelical Christian, and to oppose
failure to give the individual the place of priority to which he is
due in help for his needs. At this point our third treatment of this
crucial concept has to do with keeping it central in helping
people.

If there is one secular profession more apparently concerned for the centrality of the individual than any other such profession, it is social work.

However, we need to note that the population explosion, with its consequent strains and stresses, has alarmed many of today's sociologists and social workers, among others. It is at least one reason for such thinkers' abandoning a vital view of the welfare of the individual as indispensable to the welfare of the group. "Traditionally the Christian Church has devoted its major resources to the evangelization of individuals. But recently, a number of church leaders, both ministers and laymen, have embarked upon a campaign to persuade the churches to use their resources to bring about a social revolution . . . some churchmen have enthusiastically proposed that social revolution become the primary task of the Church in our times." [8]

Christians should look at the current discussion of violence so as to see what violence *is* telling us, as well as to see what some observers *say* it is telling us. The implication of the quotation by Professor Ilion T. Jones is that a social revolution has to do with changing groups, conceived of as masses of people rather than as individuals. This is said similarly in Peter Wagner's survey of the Latin-American scene: "The changing of the structures of society, and not the proclamation of a message to win converts, should be the true evangelistic burden of today's Church." [9] Thus, mesmerism with a desired social end causes rejection of the only event (conversion of an individual to Christ by the operation of the Holy Spirit) which, multiplied by many conversions of individuals, can ever be expected to have an eternally abiding outcome in human lives. Operating properly, the converted ones then work within their own religious organizations to help one another with their temporal problems to whatever degree is possible within the limits of their resources. They also work with others in the community toward problem solving in the community. This is the way the evangelicals ought to go about changing social structures under normal circumstances.

Approaching this from another angle, we note that there are theorists today in religious and social welfare circles, who assume that there is something archaic and even evil about too much preoccupation with the individual. It is inefficient, they say, to have an individual possessor of goods (one of the *haves*) feel individually responsible to be *his brother's keeper* and do good to a person who was one of the *have nots* in destitute circumstances. This, say such theorists, gives the impression that individuals, who are regarded as inferior due to their low economic and social status, are subservient to those *above* them. They prefer to think of dealing with people in the mass, in new developmental programs, including prevention; in public health, educational, and mental health programs, for instance. They are enamored, for good or ill, with providing more and more social insurances and sharing of wealth, and with the government becoming less and less involved in purely economic issues and more involved in the provision of welfare aid for the *masses.*

It is not necessary for the evangelical to be opposed to programs of the kind mentioned above. The programs may be good or bad on their own merits, and worthy or not worthy of his support. The critical issue is that of evangelical responsibility to keep focus on the individual. The evangelical knows that state domination of the individual should he become submerged in the mass could result in the obliteration of most individual liberties.

The Welfare State and the Individual

When welfare programs are good, they ought not be condemned just because they are large, or governmentally administered. All Americans, evangelicals included, should come to realize that the welfare state is with us, as is a welfare world. The impartial minister to human needs, as the evangelical should be, may spend time in private, and occasionally in public, opposing or defending the welfare state according to his own opinions. However, when the Christian is functioning as a witness for Christ and a minister to human needs, he must realize as a fact that the welfare state is a fact of life that affects us all. We need not concern ourselves with whether or not we want it to come into being, for it has already come into real enough being. What we are obliged to do is help people in need within this real situation. We must do it for all individuals in need, *on welfare* or not.

Proper Group Action

In referring to helping individuals and doing so in welfare settings, we cannot fail to realize that group action of the proper kind is necessary. This is true in any group needs if large numbers of people are to be successfully served.

We have here another instance of an issue not being that of either/or but that of both/and. *Proper* group action *is* essential, every bit as much as proper individual care. The Scriptures remind us that "none of us liveth to himself, and no man dieth to himself." [10] Each individual must be concerned with his relationship to each group in which he is a member. This is true of his family, his school group, work associates, church organization, and more.

True group concern for each individual in it is the reciprocal side of this essential relationship. We will be seeing this later in connection with the Christian in his local church.

A proper emphasis on the individual is actually in the very best interest of groups. The very essence of the methods used in intergroup relations is to be very sensitive to the needs of each individual in each group. Social group work method focuses on the use of the group as a medium through which to provide service for each individual in the group. Community organization techniques in social work have the same purpose.

As long as group focus is not contaminated by belittling of the individual, then plans and programs and services for the group are very much in order and are being called for more as time goes on.

References for Chapter 16

1. *Encyclopedia of Social Work* (1965), articles *in loco:* pp. 130–137; 418–428; 587–595.
2. Genesis 2:18. (Sociologically speaking, a group is composed of two persons or more.)
3. "Religious Content in Social Work Education," *Workshop Report, 1960 Proceedings, Annual Program Meeting,* Council on Social Work Education, *passim,* especially Harriet MacLaurin and Arnulf M. Pins on "What Specific Content on Religion Should Be Included and Where Should It Come?" pp. 49–70.
4. Alan R. Gruber, "Religion and Social Work," *Journal of the American Scientific Affiliation,* Vol. 18, No. 2 (June, 1966), pp. 33–35.
5. Herbert Stroup, "The Common Predicament of Religion and Social Work," *Social Work,* Vol. 7, No. 2 (April, 1962), pp. 92, 93.
6. Werner W. Boehm, "Relationship of Social Work to Other Professions," *Encyclopedia of Social Work* (1965), pp. 640–648.
7. Charles G. Chakerian, "Religious Sponsorship," *Ibid.,* pp. 654–660.
8. Ilion T. Jones, "The Church's Defection from a Divine Mission," *Christianity Today,* Vol. XII, No. 17 (May 24, 1968), p. 3.
9. C. Peter Wagner, "Evangelism and Social Action in Latin America," *Christianity Today,* Vol. X, No. 7 (January 7, 1966), p. 10.
10. Romans 14:7.

17

Evangelical Christian Social Work

Christian Participation in Social Services

Long before there were social welfare services in the ways
they are organized today under such a designation, the multiple
activities of providing *charity* were chiefly centered in the Church.
Governmental auspices before the twentieth century were minimal compared to what they are now. Religious and other private
sponsorship was of key importance because governmental provisions for human need were nonexistent or inadequate.

As government help became more necessary, especially in the
larger cities, religious and other private agencies joined tax-
supported facilities in the one common cause of meeting burgeon-
ing welfare demands. Churches that were divergent doctrinally
from one another collaborated in relief of human suffering as
they cooperated in social service activity. Before public schools
were universal and before the introduction of both private and
government-sponsored programs of reading, sewing, cooking,
language classes, and much more, pastors and church visitors
were busy in home visitation. More than one home missionary
and colportage ministry was begun in urban centers as well as
in rural areas by workers who spread the Scriptures and visited
in the homes of the slums, the prairies and the mountains, the
forests and the farms.

One such example is that of the first days of the Moody Bible Institute of Chicago and of the Moody Church. Workers visited families, distributed the Scriptures, and invited them to Sunday school and to sewing classes and other special activities, including day school.[1]

City rescue missions joined many churches and early Bible institutes across the country in conducting classes in reading, writing, the study of English, and in several special interests, not forgetting to include recreational activities when facilities were available.

Activities of this kind were the forerunners of practical Christian work and Christian service ministries continuing to the present day. These ministries, such as those at the Philadelphia School of the Bible and the Bible Institute of Pennsylvania (now merged as Philadelphia College of Bible), and others of the more than two hundred sixty Bible institutes and Bible colleges across the country, are in many instances being updated methods-wise to reach today's generation for Christ. In most such institutions, no dilution of the Message is taking place.

There have always been the spiritually, physically, and materially needy to be ministered to, and students and staff in those early days combined to deliver much help not available from any other source. Such workers for the most part had no way to get training in advanced methods of doing social welfare work even if they wanted to do so. Their service ministries were integrated with their class instruction, which is even more so today. Sometimes they reached lives which welfare functionaries could not touch. Sometimes they were handicapped by not having the knowledge and use of social welfare techniques. Above all, the evangelical, then and now, has been known for his spreading of the life-changing Word of God. Accordingly, that Bible school which should ever change its message in order to use methods which could not be used without such a change would no longer be evangelical nor a Bible school in the evangelical sense.

Dwight L. Moody and the Needs of the People

When Dwight L. Moody, one of the founding fathers of the Bible college movement, was asked his philosophy and program for the founding of the Moody Bible Institute, he placed between a practical mastery of the English Bible and the study of music the following: "Second, I would have workers trained in everything that will give them access practically to the souls of the people, especially the neglected classes." [2] There is no doubt in this writer's mind that, if Mr. Moody were alive today, he would interest himself in the best use of acceptable social work methods of latest development. He would see that as necessary to helping multitudes by means of sectarian social work in the form of evangelical Christian social work. In his own day, he knew how to include among his methods a community relations factor which did not compromise his own position, made a positive Christian witness in addition, and gave him openings to help people in spiritual and material need.

New Awareness by Evangelicals

Evangelicals have felt that doctrinal compromise with social gospel advocates and secular welfare influences have justified them in engaging in welfare activities mainly within their own circles. Little by little in the mid-fifties and with a rush in the late sixties, evangelicals have become aware that they can and must work with community agencies to help the myriads of people in need.

Evangelicals are beginning to find that they can contribute

to community life and that they are not forced to compromise their own spiritual witness in so doing, when they know what to expect in relationships with the community which knows them in return. This they can corroborate by asking evangelicals who are experienced in working with the community.

Christian social workers, inner city leaders of churches, Bible school and Sunday school program directors, and rescue mission superintendents would in some instances be very helpful to fellow evangelicals in stimulation of new and needed ministries. *In some instances* is a necessary phrase because many such persons and/or their boards of trustees and/or their constituencies are resistive of change for a number of reasons, some of them justifiable. If there were only some way of evangelical churches availing themselves of the vast assets of all evangelical inner city installations, including both human assets and property and equipment, a mighty movement could get a great impetus through the awakening of such a sleeping giant!

Church Social Service Ministries

Outside such ministries as those of an occasional or special kind by churches or through rescue missions, literature distributors and Christian social agencies, churches in recent decades did not and do not ordinarily extend their own social service ministries beyond their own congregational borders for three main reasons.

First, doctrinal reasons make them feel they do not have enough identity of purpose and method in common with nonreligious social workers and secular social work agencies to warrant collaboration with them.

Second, the church workers often sincerely believe themselves unable to compare in methods with the professional workers in the work they do that is parallel to that of church social service.

Third, in many cases, the church worker simply does not know how to go about doing most social work efficiently.

One thing is sure: The crises of today dictate that all social workers, religious and secular, be joined by Christian workers of every kind, to collaborate in coping with the present explosion of needs and problems. To refuse to do what is in our power under God to do is to be inhumane and insensitive to human suffering. There also are opportunities for spiritual ministrations accompanying religious social service which are unparalleled in the past or until now.

It is almost impossible for church pastors and other workers to do a thorough piece of work in counseling people in need without knowing at least a minimum amount of information about facilities available in the community to help them. This includes medical, social welfare, and educational resources. Many church personnel do not know these facilities because they have not had opportunity to learn about them. The example of a denominational leader in not knowing of the fifty-year existence of a central planning agency to facilitate community action against social problems in his own area is duplicable many times over.

In some evangelical Christian institutions there is sincere interest in the inclusion of suitable training in social service methods, but, "There is no room in the curriculum" or "There is no provision in our budget for it."

It is most striking to note that many denominations and individual churches will (and so they should) send missionaries abroad, teaching them to do the equivalent of social welfare work there along with nursing, teaching, building, farming—and at the same time these same auspices will not prepare Christian workers here to do social work to assist their harried pastors.

It is not an either/or issue, it is a matter of both/and. We are to give the Word of God both at home and abroad, in every instance possible, and whether or not we have anything else to give, such as food, clothing, shelter, employment. But when we *do* have other things to give, we are to give them in Jesus' Name. We are to give such help as part of a complete ministry to the whole man.[3]

As part of our functioning better in helping, we need in the very least to familiarize ourselves with (1) ways of helping people in emergencies; (2) all available community facilities and what they have to offer, such as police, fire, hospital, medical, social welfare and emergency organizations (as, American Red Cross), and liaison arrangements with them; and, where there are any, (3) evangelical Christian social agencies and any churches with social work programs for the elderly, day care centers for all ages, and much more.

It used to be that one church or several churches would band together if they saw a need to organize some Christian gospel center or mission outside the churches themselves. Up until about the nineteen twenties, all that interested people had to do when they wanted to launch a project to help people in need was to get some resources and like-minded people together, organize in some informal way to do the job, and go to work at it.

Now, by the nineteen seventies, it is increasingly necessary for most people taking the lead in social service ministries to be formally recognized in the community. This may be by being a volunteer in community service and recognized by the agency for service given. For increasing numbers of people, this will mean securing social work education on the master's or bachelor's degree levels in order to be allowed to carry on even some of the most basic ministries to help people. There are now some courses for several types of community service or community health workers which can be taken by high school graduates. There are community college courses springing up all over the country in which many students are taking the associate in arts courses, including some in social welfare.

Understanding Citizens of the Welfare State

We noted earlier that we are in a welfare world, to some extent. We ought to realize the vital need for church-connected workers to understand people who are on welfare. We should learn their feelings about being on welfare and how they are affected by welfare policies and practices.

As Missionary Richard Metzger remarked in the Spring of 1968 in a course at Philadelphia College of Bible, "You cannot serve God while ignoring men." Ignorance may not be wilful ignoring, but continued lack of better knowledge of people's needs on the part of evangelical Christians will constitute ignoring if we do not avail ourselves of ways of correcting such abuse.

We neither oppose nor endorse the welfare state, no more than we oppose or endorse the air we breathe. We are in the real situation of dealing with it as a fact of life, and minister to people who are in it with us.

We insist that being properly subject to "the powers that be" [4] and "Render . . . unto Caesar the things which are Caesar's" [5] include at least knowing what governmental welfare laws are in force and what consequent welfare policies and operations are prescribed. It is most disturbing to note that some religious institutions do not even realize that to disagree with some welfare programs is one thing, but to downgrade and attack good and necessary welfare provisions because of disagreeing with abuses is another.

We should not fail to secure social welfare knowledge because both in this country and in foreign lands, missionaries increasingly report that welfare regulations are increasing in quantity and in the imposition of requirements and standards for social service. Meeting welfare requirements on the mission field, as anywhere, is not only necessary but obligatory if we are to preserve a good testimony in the communities where we serve.

Increasing Regulations and Standards

A first important factor to learn concerning welfare regulations is that there are stiffer regulations and requirements to start or to continue in some fields of social service, such as children's services and group living facilities. These requirements may have to do with such things as having at least minimally acceptable physical facilities and equipment and having specified amounts of air space between and above beds in a dormitory.

The requirement which is set up in so many instances for administrators and supervisors in social agencies is that of requireing such personnel to have master's degrees or approved bachelor's degrees in social work. Institutions and agencies or departments in them have sometimes been closed or voluntarily discontinued when this requirement is not met. In such cases, some needed services cannot even be started without this standard being met in the first place. The recent recognition of a bachelor's degree earned in an undergraduate social work sequence when it has met curriculum and other specifics may well be a boon to Christian churches and agencies.

In some instances, evangelical Christian institutions have secured workers with required degrees regardless of whether or not they are evangelical Christians. In other instances, activities have been cancelled and agencies closed rather than the agencies in question hiring nonevangelicals due to the shortage of evangelicals with proper credentials.

This is not a time to question whether the requirements are just or necessary. What is needed is to realize that most regulations that are put into effect protect the evangelicals, too, since higher standards usually result in better service in the long run. What counts now is that new standards are put into effect *as law,* and are to be met regardless of our feelings about them. We must meet the demands of the law in order to minister to many we cannot help otherwise—and we keep the law because wanting to keep the law is characteristic of those who believe in the rule of law as do evangelicals.

Even stricter requirements will be forthcoming. Licensing of many more agencies which provide social service will probably take place, and regulations set up governing more services provided in them. Licensing of social workers might become nation-wide instead of existing in only a few states and smaller localities. There will be several levels of workers, from professionals to volunteers, as now. However, all workers, even most volunteers, will have more thorough training.

Another side of the social welfare scene is the fact that more and more social services are likely to be coordinated and controlled centrally from state and federal centers. Automation and computerization of records will facilitate welfare services.

The evangelical student of social action in this age prepares himself by studying the seedbed of beneficial social action, the Bible, and learns social welfare and social work to whatever degree is necessary for his individual ministry in this generation.

Illustration of a Suggested Program of Preparation

What can be done to school people for this type of Christian ministry?

Curricula can be devised and taken like the one offered since 1965 at Philadelphia College of Bible. It is called the Bible Social Work Major. It is not the first program of its kind in colleges in general or in Christian colleges. It *is* believed to be the first of its kind so fully developed in a specifically *Bible college* setting. It is part of a development in recent years of undergraduate social welfare education in many colleges across the nation. There have been a few courses in colleges for a long time on the introduction to social welfare and social work. This newer program is a deliberate new thrust by many colleges who offer greater depth and connected sequences now.

As tested at Philadelphia College of Bible, the first seven years of the program have proved effective in preparing students to work among the needy. Graduates are serving in evangelical social service, other social welfare posts, inner city and home and foreign mission ministries, and in graduate schools and seminaries training for future service.

Curriculum and Other Preparation for Social Service Ministries

As preparation to operate to the maximum efficiency in helping people in need, the following general coverage should be made by each Christian institution wanting to gear itself to some beginning preparation for social service ministries. Whether the institution is a college, seminary, special educational center, or practical training program will determine the amount and proportion of these curriculum ingredients:

1. General liberal arts educational requirements.

2. Studies in the behavioral sciences, especially those most helpful to the understanding of people and their social needs and problems.

3. Courses about or in the field of social welfare and social work.

4. Practical work of some kind, as social field work, supervised and in conjunction with class work.

Along with the foregoing, there is the indispensable constellation of studies in the Scriptures and in evangelization, with focus on use in religious settings, churches, and missionary settings of all kinds:

1. Study of the Bible in large quantity and depth, in application to life, and in relation to its use with helping methods.

2. Separate or combined studies in Church history and present state of the Church, revivals and great awakenings, missionary methods, evangelism, Christian education, and the effect of God's Word and God's people on social conditions in the past and present.

References for Chapter 17

1. Bernard R. DeRemer, *Moody Bible Institute: A Pictorial History* (Chicago, Moody Press, 1960), pp. 21–27.
2. *Ibid.*, p. 30.
3. Proverbs 3:27, 28; James 2:14–26, et al.
4. Romans 13:1.
5. Matthew 22:21.

18

Our Debt to All Men

Author's Fear

The author fears that many of his fellow evangelicals might give lip service, and sincere lip service backed up with intentions to match, to the idea that all people in need ought to be helped. He fears that they might not trouble themselves to particularize, however, by following up their good wishes for the poor with appropriate action.

If the Christian truly believes that he has a social responsibility to discharge along with a responsibility for the spiritual welfare of men, he will not be in the category described as follows: "Today we live in a world of revolutionary change and unparalleled challenge, and the task is now before organized Christianity to minister to the needs of modern man. Unfortunately, altogether too many evangelicals are more concerned with their own status in society, and they find themselves in the position of either opposing social change or at least ignoring it. These people live in a segmented, compartmentalized world in which the Christian faith has only to do with one's internal well-being and posthistorical destiny." [1]

Rather than this, the Christian will cast about him to see what needs to be done for others as the Lord leads. The burden of the remainder of this book must be more suggestions for Christian action than we have considered so far.

When the Christian acknowledges that some forms of social action would be contrary to God's will, he understandably asks, "What strengths and equipment, what strategies and tactics are ours to use?"

Counting Our Strengths and Equipment

Beginning with a bit of recapitulation of some assets we have listed before, we can go quickly into further advantages. Needless to say except to be sure we do not take it for granted, we see the gospel message itself which we are to convey to others. The cure for many of the basic difficulties underlying social problems is sin and the gospel is good news that there is a Saviour from sin. Our debt to all men [2] is to reach them with the glad tidings of salvation. "Riots broke out," writes Evangelist Tom Skinner. "And I knew that the only answer to these social problems was a direct confrontation involving all people of all races with Jesus Christ." [3]

Prayer

One of the forces available to us is prayer. Prayer is communication with God. Prayer engaged in by members of a group includes the interaction of the group's members and is thus also a social act. Prayer together in the Holy Spirit can and does affect attitudes toward people in need, toward people of different racial and social identities, and toward doing God's will in truly Christian social action.

Social Concern

Prayer in part grows out of social concern. The term social concern should be scrapped, unless it is used to designate the driving force which spurs to action and is not a sentimental substitute for action.

Social concern is a point beyond which some individuals will not go, even though they do not admit to themselves that they limit themselves in this way. They do not want to go beyond concern to *action*. They sometimes do not really want to improve the lot of anyone if the improvement of that person's situation will pose any threat to their own power or possessions.

Another side to a spurious social concern is that it is often a condescending attitude of people who do not mean to seem superior but unconsciously feel so toward people they consider inferior—and the *inferior* ones get the message!

Love

Concern at its best is one of the attributes of the greatest force of all for social action: Love. The Scriptures tell us to "Owe no man any thing, but to love one another." [4] (Note that the last half of the verse couples love and law and does not pit love against law in a spurious and fictitious alliance of love with justice: "for he that loveth another hath fulfilled the law.")

Exhortation to love is manifestly not new. Yet, we submit that there is a model of Christian love for the nineteen seventies that needs unveiling. It is an aspect of Christian love that has been included in it all along, but one which needs special prominence in the current crisis. Consider it this way: We have often heard it said that a person can *love* another person but not *like* him. The model for the nineteen seventies and beyond if the Lord gives longer time is, one must love *and* like another, as much as possible, with God's help. It is true that there are individual differences which cause difficulty of one person's even getting along with another. Christian love can be the individual spirit of one person relating with another person with the love of God making this relationship what none of the loves of this world can do. If the individual is not a Christian, the love of God is sharpened in the believer's heart into a love of solicitation for the person in need—including solicitation that that person come to God through Christ. If the person is a Christian, the bond of Christian love already formed operates to grow stronger, and to apply to any particular circumstances in which there may be the need for the exercise of love.

Peace

Peace is another word the world uses constantly. As in the case of love, the Christian needs clear understanding of what it means to him so he can use it precisely.

Evangelicals could not be forced into a uniform stand on world peace in this age, since some evangelicals believe some degree of it is achievable now and others believe no significant amount of tranquility can be retrieved now.

The Christian's expectation of the Prince of Peace's imposing peace on earth at His second coming has as its forerunner today the inner peace known by those who have accepted Jesus as Saviour. He is the one born "in the city of David a Saviour, which is Christ the Lord," to those who enjoy peace on earth to men having a good will (toward God). [5] This person who is thus in a right relationship with God must attend well to his relationships with men.

The Christian is exhorted to pursue peace with all men,[6] showing that peace claims not a minor place in the individual's advance in the Christian life, but a major one. Companion action with the Christian's outward working at peaceful living is the inner progress of the peace of God planted in his heart by the Holy Spirit. The word *pursue* is a strong and self-explanatory one. It is well-related to another exhortation of God to the Christian to concentrate on the better conduct of his relations with others as he submits to the fruits of the Spirit of God working through him.[7]

Pursuing peace does not rule out taking a stand for one's own rights or the rights of others. It does include taking into account the limitations of human personalities and the infinite number of differences there are among people: "If it be possible, as much as lieth in you, live peaceably with all men." [8]

Unity

Evangelical unity might seem like a strange concept to someone who remembers the impossibility of uniting evangelicals in matters where there is so great a latitude for permissible differences of views, such as in the peace issue.

Let not the inquirer be deflected from seeing evangelicals too much differently from what they really prove to be at a closer look. Evangelicals insist, because the Bible insists, on the right of individuals and of local churches and larger church bodies to differ on many particulars.

It is therefore important that any evangelical disunity be correctly estimated. It is only peripheral disunity, and not deep. In the many areas in which wide latitude of opinion and practice is possible, evangelicals rejoice in such freedom. On God's call to all men to come to him through Christ [9] and other essentials, unity of belief is enjoyed in the true ecumenicity believers have had through the ages, and is to be cultivated in love and peace. [10] As the motionless depths of the sea are below the storm-lashed surface, so the oneness in the faith [11] is not disturbed by surface differences of the evangelicals.

Differences and Divisions

There are some groups among evangelicals, and some individuals, who cannot work with other evangelicals in some ways and for various reasons. One mark of a spiritual revival is that during such spiritual refreshing many of these differences are dissolved or overlooked. Between such periods of refreshing, the limitations of human knowledge and personality factors accentuate the differences. The crises of our day wring from us the cry of the Psalmist, "It is time for thee, Lord, to work: for they have made void thy law." [12] They should also urge from us the call of the Prophet which needs re-emphasis in our day: "it is time to seek the Lord!" [13] The same crises capped by the unrighteousness about us should cause us to challenge one another with, "Awake to righteousness, and sin not; for some have not the knowledge of God." [14]

Evangelicals were arguing to preserve essentials when the world's population was approaching the two billion mark, and are properly concerned about essential faith and practice as we approach four billion on earth. Will we still be preserving essentials when the population reaches nearly the seven billion mark about A.D. 2000?

The answer is that we probably will be doing so, or at least some of us will. We must have some appointed to tend to matters of sound doctrine, and the defense of it. But what about the majority of us?

We must continue to contend for the essentials of the faith [15] and at the same time put aside cavils and quibbling about lesser things in the present atmosphere of threatened world catastrophe. We who know God's safety and security [16] must major in action—using all appropriate methods to bring others to the same Rock of Salvation we have.

When Jeremiah was called to the prophet's office, God specified that he was "to build, and to plant." [17] Before he was to be constructive, however, he was to be faithfully destructive; he was told to "root out, and to pull down, and to destroy, and to throw down." [18] In applying this principle today, we can believe that carnal divisiveness among evangelical brethren might be torn down and a good relationship put in its place.

This is the same issue faced by Paul as he addressed the Corinthians about it: "I beseech you . . . that there be no divisions among you . . . there are contentions among you . . . every one of you saith, I am of Paul; and I of Apollos; and I of Cephas; and I of Christ. Is Christ divided? . . . I determined not to know any thing among you, save Jesus Christ, and him crucified." [19]

Paul's rebuke of giving prime allegiance to a human leader rather than to Christ and his exhortation to the divided groups to unite under Christ are eminently appropriate for today. If individual Christians find themselves more comfortable under a strong leader of a movement, let them be sure to be followers of such a leader in the way Paul says in the same epistle: "Be ye followers of me, even as I also am of Christ." [20] Let such individuals be sure their leader is truly exalting Christ rather than self. The insistence we make on understanding divisions among ourselves is made so that we may the better concentrate on achieving greater unity among evangelicals, with the manifest purpose of ministering more effectively to the needs of humanity.

Assuming that all evangelical groups agree basically on doctrinal grounds, divisions among evangelicals ought to be understood in part as follows:

First, Jesus did not insist on formal union as long as the message proclaimed by others was identical with that of Jesus' own followers: "Master, we saw one casting out devils in thy name; and we forbad him, because he followeth not with us. And Jesus said unto him, Forbid him not: for he that is not against us is for us." [21]

In the second case, all evangelicals who can comfortably do so should be united in fellowship and mutual Christian service ministries, including ministrations to the needy wherever possible.

This may be done in groups which are formally united with one another or by informal organizations.

A third aspect of this factor of division has to do with those evangelicals who insist on being separate from the rest to the point of withholding fellowship from them. They are still obliged to God to maintain proclamation of the one message of the one Saviour, thus, speaking the same thing.[22]

Church and Society

Looking at the relationships of church and society, we ask first about the political realm. The oft-argued question of whether and how Christians should take a stand on political issues calls for caution: "More and more, Christians are called upon to join crusades to promote white supremacy, freedom riders, anti-Communism, civil liberties, laissez-faire economics, Christian socialism, constitutional government, pacifism, militarism, and a host of other causes. Public relations experts pushing these causes use Scripture references, names of respected Christian leaders, and other devices. They convey the impression that every sincere Christian ought to support their movement, agency, or organization. Christians need always to remember, however, that not all who quote the Bible are truly scriptural." [23]

While we cannot dictate to the individual Christian conscience that there must or must not be positions for or against social action issues by direct statement on the part of a church or group of churches, it must be urged that evangelical Christians take a stand on vital issues wherever and however possible. One view is:

"We as Christians must believe and adhere personally to the standards we know to be Bible-based. We ought also to declare to the world in any united way open to us that we take this or that position for or against political, socioeconomic, religious, educational, and any other issues. We ought to declare such positions only after we ascertain their scriptural validity. We ought *not* do this because we believe that by so doing we can bring about a type of 'righteousness' wherein each individual who obeys such directives becomes personally righteous in the sight of God. Nor should we intimate that we can banish the world's evils thus. We *should* do this because we believe these are the conditions under which we want our own Christian constituency to live; we testify that these are the positions upon which all men's lives should be based; and we know that by such declarations God might be pleased to use our testimony in His restraining common grace shed upon all men." [24]

Another angle from which to view this question is that which we shall call cultural humility. Refusal to take any stand on social and other community problems is often said to be refusal on scriptural grounds, those of having no fellowship with unbelievers. If this is a really sincere position, we must defend a person's right to it. Is it possible, however, that some who take this position might take it out of the convenience it affords to avoid thought and action on pressing issues of the day?

Is it possible that some evangelical reluctance to be involved in social issues might stem from pique and embarrassment because evangelicals are no longer in many places of prominence and control over society and social action now?

God's Daily Leading

The key to taking a stand on vital issues of any kind, community problems or otherwise, is the leading of the Holy Spirit in the life of the Christian each day as He leads in accordance with the Scriptures.

As the Christian is led to be vocal and visible in his community, he increases the likelihood that others might listen when he has an opportunity to speak a word about Jesus. "Apart from denominational problems, it remains that the true evangelical, in the very proportion that the culture in which he lives is not actually Christian, must unite with nonevangelicals for social betterment if it is to be achieved at all, simply because the evangelical forces do not predominate. To say that evangelicalism should not voice its convictions in a nonevangelical environment is simply to rob evangelicalism of its missionary vision." [25]

Note the seriousness of indifference to the circumstances of life, as they affect the neighbors of Christians: "How can you love a person and neglect his physical welfare? . . . by neglecting the body we have to a large extent forfeited the right to be heard. People just will not listen to us until they are convinced we are concerned about their bodies as well as their souls." [26]

Our debt to all men to deliver the gospel to them, then, includes winning their confidence when God makes it possible. Once they have some degree of confidence, perhaps they will get a glimpse of our love for them, and God's love through us.

References for Chapter 18

1. Clouse, et al., *Protest and Politics*, p. 3.
2. Romans 1:14.
3. Tom Skinner, *Black and Free* (Grand Rapids, Zondervan Publishing House, 1968), p. 125.
4. Romans 13:8.
5. Luke 2:11, 14.
6. Hebrews 12:14.
7. Galatians 5:22, 23.
8. Romans 12:18.
9. Ezekiel 18:23, 32; 2 Corinthians 5:17–21.
10. Ephesians 4:1–3.
11. Ephesians 4:4–6.
12. Psalms 119:126.
13. Hosea 10:12.
14. 1 Corinthians 15:34.

15. Jude 3.
16. Isaiah 30:15; 32:17.
17. Jeremiah 1:10.
18. *Idem.*
19. 1 Corinthians 1:10–13; 2:2.
20. 1 Corinthians 11:1.
21. Luke 9:49, 50.
22. 1 Corinthians 1:10.
23. Moberg, *Christian Social Responsibility*, p. 23.
24. Charles Y. Furness, address, "Morality and the Changing Social Structure," Annual Convention, National Association of Evangelicals (April 25, 1968), *typed*, p. 6.
25. Henry, *Uneasy Conscience*, p. 80.
26. Fred A. Alexander, "Christ Is Not the Answer! Or Is Christ Really the Answer?" *Freedom Now* (May–June, 1968), p. 9.

19

The Local Church,
Center of Operations

Primacy of the Church

Each local church group of believers is God's key unit in the community for His kind of social action as well as for the other functions of the church body.

The church assembles to worship, to have fellowship with one another as believers in Christ, to keep the ordinances of the Lord's Supper and baptism and—to evangelize!

Priority of the Word

The proclamation of the Word of God holds top priority and the place of central importance in the church. It is the source of God's impartation of truth to Christians, and it incorporates the message they proclaim to the world. While the church may be concerned for people so as to minister to their needs, the church takes care that methods of such ministry do not hinder the transmission of the message of God. Any social action called Christian which in any way is likely to obscure or replace the outflow of the good news of God is properly suspect. Truly Christian social action flows out from preaching the Word as a proper sequel to the ministry of the Word.[1]

A search of the Scriptures shows individual changes of lives

214

in the local churches, which resulted from the operation of God's Word in human hearts.[2]

The same is true today. Individually, lives are changed and then become reproductive as each transmits the transforming gospel to others.[3] Secular social action, not stemming from manifestly Christian results of the operation of God the Holy Spirit in and through believers, must be analyzed in the light of the Scriptures to ascertain if it is at all in conformity to what God would approve in accordance with His Scriptures.

This concern for things being done God's way is inherent in both Old and New Testaments. David learned the hard way not to do things impulsively and with a desire to be like other people. He failed to follow God's directions on how to perform an act of worship the right way, especially since God had already specified how such an act was to be performed. He had tried to do a good thing in restoring the ark of the covenant to a place of prominence without even realizing he was doing it in an evil way. God was displeased, and David had to bring the ark up to Jerusalem in the way God prescribed.[4]

It is no wonder that the evangelical is concerned because he sees that so often men are trying to help other men in ways which might not be in accordance with God's will. He shrinks from using methods by which he would seem to help God out as if he thought God's power were limited.

True improvement of social conditions flows out of Biblical influence. Evangelist Graham says: "I am convinced that if the church went back to its main task of preaching the gospel and getting people converted to Christ it would have far more impact on the social structure of the nation than it can have in any other thing it could possibly do." [5] Good works, of which evangelical Christian social action is a part, flow out of faith which in turn results from hearing the gospel.

Planning How to Reach the People

The question is, What does God want done to spread the gospel? Is it too risky to try to preach the gospel in exposed places and explosive situations? Is it possible to set up procedures which will work everywhere or is it necessary to wait for each situation to dictate strategy and methods?

Whatever the proper methods, wherever used, the overriding motivation of the Christian is: "I am made all things to all men, that I might by all means save some. And this I do for the gospel's sake." [6] This being so, once he is sure the "all things" he does are pleasing to God, the evangelical is one of the first to launch into an approach to the people so as to give the gospel message. This explains why, once so convinced, the evangelical enters social work activities so as to show his sensitiveness to all human need and this in turn often opens the door to help him "save some."

In these days of people going out in the open to demonstrate something or another to the public, evangelical Christians ought surely to seek acceptable opportunities to present the gospel in places of public assemblage or through news media. They should feel compelled to *make* such opportunities as God leads.

There is one opportunity which needs pondering and calls for action, once evangelicals are sure how to do it in today's context. This is the opportunity of reaching people in the open air. Methods may include:

1. Conventional open-air preaching methods.

2. Deliberate formation of a *demonstration* technique, including appropriate use of special trucks and communications media, taking the gospel to people in places and by methods where *conventional* methods are not always possible or would be likely to be rejected. Always, evangelicals must know and obey all per-

tinent laws and regulations, and collaborate with the authorities in keeping the peace. These latter stipulations are essential parts of a permissible demonstration along with the use of properly aggressive but acceptable methods. This is part of what is involved in action "in demonstration of the Spirit and of power." [7]

3. Development of *task force* techniques of individual and group readiness to insert gospel witnessing appropriately at moments of emergency or crisis.

Again it is not either/or; it is both/and. We are culturally bound always to setting up a time, and a place, to expect people to attend scheduled services. This we must continue to do whether in church, in private home, or elsewhere. We should also develop *minute men* and *commando* tactics of application of God's Word to today's ills, anywhere, as occasion arises on short notice or unexpectedly.

The Local Church Base

It is no strange idea to the evangelical that the local church is thought of as the center of activity for the congregation and the launching pad from which Christians go forth to proclaim Christ. It is also the place to which the Christians bring God's converts for strengthening in the faith and to become a working part of the body of *called-out ones*, along with those who have contacted them for Christ.

Much is made these days of getting people into group situations so they might benefit therapeutically from interaction with group members. Likewise, if done properly, bringing others in some way into contact with the local church may result in leading them to Christ. This gets them into a group situation with the church in which they are bound to profit for the present and for eternity. As long as each individual looks to the Lord Jesus and not to the members of the group for ultimate satisfaction, the individual who comes to Christ will get the most important experience of all that is available in the church. This is the strengthening through fellowship with other Christians of his already-begun connection with them through the mutual faith they have in Christ.

Also, the individual who has brought a new individual into the church and the one brought in continue to work together to make Christ known. It is essential for both evangelism and evangelical Christian social action that individual members be provided with adequate preparation to witness for Christ wherever God puts them.

With adequate Christian education by the local church and related educational bodies, the individual evangelical church member is a vital force for God today, and, joined with others as a group, is a potential for action second to none when energized by the Holy Spirit.

The Local Church Basic

The individual church member is rightly concerned for the local church. He knows it is the key group for God today. He knows it to be his responsibility to keep its doctrine and practice sound. He wonders if the church's increased participation in Christian social service outreach will dilute the evangelistic outreach of the church. He also wonders if the bringing in of additional people to attend church, or even to go so far as to become members, will alter the spiritual equilibrium of the body.

The individual who comes into the local fellowship ought not to be discouraged from entrance into the membership soon, if he comes on scriptural grounds. Nor should he be encouraged to join soon if he is not ready. Be he white, black, young, old, rich, poor, he should not be received into membership until he is ready.

In many foreign mission field situations, it is necessary to have candidates for church membership kept in a preparatory stage over many months or even a year or more so as to help the new convert in his growth in the Christian life, and in his acculturation into the evangelical Christian subculture. Acculturation into a church in the sense used here does not mean into categories of white or black, lower or middle or upper class, poor or rich. It means acculturation into the company of true believers in Christ, of whatever composition otherwise.

Unless the local church specifies an express period of preparatory or probationary membership, the time before entrance into church membership ought to be long or short not only in keeping with the new member's own development in the Christian life, but also in the light of how ready the members of the church are to receive the new members. A person who is already a member of the same or similar subculture as most other members of the church, and who is in this way well adjusted to them, might well join soon if spiritual conditions permit. Someone quite different, like a formerly habitual alcoholic or a member of a minority group very different culturally, ought to be dealt with over a longer period of time. This is in order for the church to be reasonably sure that he has truly sought the Lord and is grounded in the fundamentals of the Christian faith. This also gives the prospective member time to be sure that this is the group of believers in which the Lord wants him to be.

Likewise, if such very different people are ready at an earlier time, the problem is not so much their being received into membership as the membership's being ready to receive them. Most evangelicals have been theoretically in accord with the principle of receiving "whosoever will" as long as the Lord has received him first. Too often it is a matter of receiving whosoever is of the same social class or race.

It is a new thing for many evangelicals to see that some people quite different from themselves, except for faith in Christ, are actually coming to the church and seeking acceptance. It surprises some that entire congregations of people different from themselves, except for identity of faith, can organize and operate their own evangelical church. This is a time of adjustment of many minds to new patterns, and members of Christian churches who are members of racial and ethnic minorities will need to have patience with majority group members who are adjusting.

As evangelical churches welcome those who are one in Christ and who may also be very different from themselves otherwise, they will soon find them so very much the same in basic personality characteristics. This will be so if love is the controlling measure used rather than cultural differences or personal preferences and prejudices.

Evangelical churches will resist tokenism or fawning paternalism to gain favor of any groups who put pressure on the churches to receive members. They will also resist pressures to keep people out who should be in. They will adhere to the one requisite for membership regardless of sex, age, race, class, or any other distinction. The one requirement is that the new member be born again, as far as the church can ascertain. In the instance of some evangelicals who are not as insistent on a regenerate church membership as others, there may be some quicker disposition to receive new members, but not really very much more quickly, if the churches in question are evangelical in actuality.

Risking in Order to Reach

So often in American church circles the in-group membership have rejected people who were different from themselves simply because they were not to their own liking, whether this was expressly stated in a bit less stark terms or in the form of an excuse. Many churches have dwindled and died, especially in the inner city, because they have excluded people who were very different from them and had not made an attempt earlier in their history to meet the needs of such.

Failure to minister to the waves of population, whether constantly the same as the membership of inner city churches or composed of successive groups of different backgrounds, is one of the indictments to be laid against many local churches. The fact that so many of them did not even realize that this was happening is sad indeed. It must be guarded against from now on so that this failure be not perpetuated.

Churches of the inner city or anywhere else ought to examine this matter of *risking* their homogeneity and social luxury in the light of what in most cases the forbears of present evangelical church members did. The churches in former days took risks and today's successors to those churches are so used to doing so that they do not even think of themselves as doing so. Many evangelical churches regularly permit non-Christians to attend and participate in worship services, in Sunday schools, youth groups, women's groups, men's groups, musical organizations, and much more, in an attempt to contact souls for Christ and bring them further under the teaching of the Bible. From these sources church memberships are recruited.

Is it too much to ask that the local church today engage in social service ministries in order to meet the needs of people? In the instances of the organizations sponsored by the church and listed above, people who took part in them enjoyed social interaction with other people. Their personal and group needs were met. Their going into the church membership was in nature an additional and qualitatively different step. The parallel is the same in the case of those we might *reach* through Christian social services. Individuals may go beyond the stage of receiving help of such a tangible kind. As they do so, they may avail themselves of the spiritual benefits available.

It is only fair to say that some churches would have been willing to minister to the people around them but that in those instances the people were not interested in the church and what it had to offer. We know this happens. Not everyone accepted Jesus' ministry either. Our point is that there is more of a likelihood today that people around some churches may respond to interest in their basic human needs as such interest is shown by the local church. Therein lies further opportunity.

References for Chapter 19

1. 2 Timothy 3:15–17.
2. Romans 6:17–23; 1 Corinthians 6:9–11; Ephesians 2:1–10; Titus 3:3–8; et al.
3. James 1:18; Romans 10:14–17.
4. 2 Samuel 6; 1 Chronicles 15 and 16.
5. Graham, *World Aflame*, p. 182.
6. 1 Corinthians 9:22, 23.
7. 1 Corinthians 2:4.

20

The Church and Community Responsibilities

(This subject is admittedly a vast one. We shall deliberately restrict our thoughts to major subdivisions of this subject, three in number. These are: (1) the church in the community around it; (2) the church and the inner city; and (3) the recruitment of workers, whether for the community around it, the inner city, or anywhere in the whole community in need of ministry, the community which is the world.[1])

Church Ministries to the Community

Church ministries to those of their own number who are in need are not new. Deacons were appointed by the early church.[2] Pastor's funds, deacons' funds, and benevolence funds are well known among us today. The pastor encounters many material and physical problems in his visitation and counseling ministries, and uses these funds in their relief. Much more good has been done than has ever been recorded on earth, due to the large degree of confidentiality which attends many of these ministrations.

Such ministries are a form of social action. Churches have often done much to minister to the needs of their own members, and to the occasional person from the outside who might come under the reach of church auspices. There have always been some churches which have been located at the crossroads of humanity. These have had large ministries to the multitudes. Some of these developed into what are referred to as *institutional churches* like Spurgeon's Metropolitan Tabernacle, which is considered a prototype of this kind of church. Today there is emerging a further demand for program-centered activities, embracing not only the church but the community as well. Care must be taken to make all activities contain Bible content or Bible-derived material and to show the relevance of having any given program in connection with a Bible-centered church or organization.

Workers must be trained to augment the pastor's visitation ministry and the benevolent outreach of the church. Just as full-time or part-time workers are needed in church music, Christian education, and youth activities, more and more are needed for church social work personnel. Whether called social worker or minister of visitation or assistant pastor or church visitor or some other designation, there is a need for personnel to do this vital work. Preferably, such work should be done by workers with some education in social work.

Further, specific Christian social service programs should be launched as branch ministries in other locations in the inner city or neglected neighborhoods in a town or in unreached rural areas, in which contact may be begun with people in need. Depending on available facilities, such programs may be initiated at the local church itself, given adequate supervision. Publications on church benevolence ministries are beginning to include sections on church social service ministries,[3] and the use the local church ought to make of welfare facilities and other local resources. Books by evangelical writers are beginning to appear with the church and social welfare as the entire subject of the work.[4]

Whether or not there is a reservoir of evangelical Christian social service ministries and experience, each local church should feel responsibility to minister to the community in which it is located *when it is able* to make any contact at all with that community. Doing so when possible is similar to a missionary's policy of locating in a mission field and ministering to the surrounding populace as they turn to the missionary. Such contact with Christian social service is as helpful to a person in need in the homeland as it is on the foreign field.

Some large churches have social welfare committees to augment the regular church ministrations. Some combination of pastor, deacons (or their equivalent), full- or part-time social worker (by whatever title), and other laymen should serve. They can assist the church's own constituency and others in the community when others can be assisted in keeping with the church program.

The local church, in addition to knowing and occasiona using Christian and secular community agencies, including so welfare agencies, should have some contact with Christian so work consultation facilities. (Such services provided in Welfare Information Service at Philadelphia College of are one form of such consultation services.) With or without services or persons with some social work knowledge i church, the church should still concern itself with social pro in church or community and go only as far as it is wisely p to go in such cases. With such services, the ministry church is made more efficient as well as effective. One often is that the church know what other social service community might be utilized so as to make referrals It is desirable to know what duplications of social servic be found in the community and what gaps there are also

the church might be able to help provide services not available elsewhere when such services are in keeping with the over-all program of the church.

Community Involvement

We do not say that all churches should try to provide all kinds of social services. We *do* say that whatever the needs of the community might be might provide the church with open doors to the community should the church be able to assist in such needs. This assistance may be provided by the church itself or it may be by a community agency the church tells those in need about. Obvious large areas of ministry with which the church can help the community include those of delinquent and pre-delinquent youth, alcoholism, drug abuse, sexual perversions, unmarried parents, adoption and foster care, child abuse, work with the aging and intergroup relations. Counseling assists with mental health needs.

When churches have adequate facilities and supervision, deliberate attempts should be made by them to look about them in the communities in which they are, and initiate what possible programs their personnel, space, and equipment will allow.

Note: The church *must not* attempt community contact and participation beyond what programs it is able to control and supervise when such programs are sponsored and conducted by the local church. It is better to wait until facilities, staff, and program provision make such action possible. It is not only for the good of the church that this is necessary. The ones for whom the services are to be provided would not be served satisfactorily and might even be harmed without the (at least minimum) requisites for good service.

An excerpt from a pamphlet describing "Church Community Weekday Ministries" [5] issued by the Southern Baptist Convention

argues, "The radical changes which have taken place around so many churches seem to make it necessary that they find effective ways for community ministry. Weekday ministries provide the opportunity for fuller use of the church buildings, as well as the best use of the talents, interests, training and capabilities of the church men and women to meet these needs by adapting the abilities of the 'helpers' to meet the needs of the 'helped.'" This pamphlet goes on to list many activities in community service from which the local church might choose according to its capacity and the needs of its community.

A partial list includes: Education (adult education, kindergarten, literacy classes, job training, tutorial services, library services); clubs with interest for all ages; day care (preschool care, before and after school care, mature adult day care); Bible classes and visitation and evangelism; Human Welfare services, like clothing, rooms, food distribution, rent assistance, emergency help, legal assistance, dental clinics, medical clinics, counseling, contacts with Welfare, meal planning, and serving; recreation; music; special projects like sewing classes, cooking classes, ceramics, art, budget planning, help in securing jobs, photography, appliance repairs, mechanics class, carpenter shop, and much more.

In the foregoing, it might appear that the church would be attempting what the school or the neighborhood house or recreation center ordinarily do. The stark truth is that the existing educational and welfare programs are inadequate to meet all the needs. Schools, for instance, are becoming social agencies to some degree because of having to cope with many aspects of pupil behavior and home circumstances. Social agencies, in turn, are having to conduct more teaching, tutoring, and other training services. In this period of flux and turmoil, the church dare not fail to carry on what social service projects the Lord indicates; it is better to give service to the whole man including his spiritual needs.

The Inner City

If evangelical churches had ever been told that they were to plan to be mission stations when located downtown, much of the havoc wrought by some churches leaving the city might have been spared. People in the churches and in the surrounding neighborhoods did not think of the churches as missionary agencies stationed there to minister to more than their own memberships.

From this time on in our American setting there ought never again be an evangelical church that does not see itself to be a missionary station to its own community. This might include an inner city ministry which a church locates not far from itself.

These days it is fashionable in some circles for some evangelicals to beat their breasts in remorse and guilt for having forsaken the inner city. It is true that many churches and rescue missions with their pastors and missioners and social workers kept on in the city and have never left it. Yet, by and large, the Church *has* neglected the inner city in general. What is so patent on the face of it is, to many Christian laymen, city missionaries are usually not thought of as missionaries in the same way other missionaries are. Perhaps they are too close to home to seem like missionaries.

Church members who live in the inner city often decide to move out without any thought that they, the church members, are missionaries fleeing a mission field. *They* were moving in. *They* at first may have been the Germans, then the Irish, the Polish, the Italians, the Jews, the Negroes, the Mexicans, the Puerto Ricans, and so on. The typical longer-settled Americans of any national background have been motivated to keep their families better off than the immigrants, so they moved.

It is not that such a man who moved out with his family necessarily had anything against the newcomers. Whether or not he did hold anything against them, he had obligations to his own family to motivate his seeking the best situations in which his family might live. He had to move them to purer air, more pleasant surroundings, higher status neighborhoods, better schools, better housing. Uppermost in his thoughts was his family's legitimate improvement. Very few, if any, have refused to seek better things if his neighbor cannot yet have them.

In some instances individuals who move out of the city who are also evangelicals *do* at least think of moving out to help in forming a new church to evangelize people in a new suburb. Responsibility to those in the neighborhood he left behind is usually not a factor in his thinking, mainly because he has never been given a reason to think of such responsibility nor ways of discharging it.

Let us ask seriously: To what extent can an inner city church be carried on in the traditional way? In ghetto areas it is hard to compete with any religious group that is already there, in order to bring in an evangelical church, or to start one where there is no other church. In inner city areas otherwise, the population that is composed of families is mobile, staying only a short while near a church of any interest to them. Other inner city residents are aged or infirm; single individuals; fragments of families; people ethnically and linguistically not likely to feel at home in an evangelical church unless they are purposely cultivated by evangelicals; people different from the usual family-centered evangelical Christian group.

This points up another connected issue: Our churches are family-centered for the most part, and so they should be where it is possible. People that are not presently members of family groups often feel that they do not have enough money to help the church or family members. Evangelicals, by concentrating on special ministries to the people in their neighborhoods who are not in families, can perform a significant task of ministering to the inner city nonfamily individuals.

This is not to say that there are not family-centered churches in the inner city. It *is* to say that so many families flee the city when their income makes it possible to move.

There are several types of people in the inner city with some degree of permanence of residence. These include the ghetto dwellers. There are pensioners and others with regularly submarginal income who cannot afford to live in more expensive quarters.

For the most part, however, inner city dwellers are highly mobile. Even if they stay in the city, they move from place to place in it.

There are apartment building tenants in many inner city sections. They are a subculture unto themselves. Some reside therein for a long time, some move frequently.

There are regional plans in many metropolitan areas to attract residents back into the inner city areas by more attractive housing and other inducements. Attempts to get people of various economic categories to move back into the city are being met with varying degrees of success.

Are we saying that because the inner city is composed of heterogeneous populations with low family percentage and low income that churches can no longer be found or new ones organized? Not exactly. What we are saying is that ways are going to have to be found to assist evangelicals in the inner city to maintain their churches and organize new ones in instances where there are not enough families with enough income to carry on the expense of church operations. Among programs advocating establishment of new churches in inner city areas is the one of several years' operation under the Conservative Baptist Home Mission Society.

Much is suggested today about paying reparations to American blacks. An evangelical version of this should be the assistance by Christians who can afford it in material and financial ways to evangelical blacks, voluntarily given in love and through capable auspices, following scriptural patterns of "Distributing to the necessity of saints." [6]

Whatever churches can do to maintain inner city testimonies may well be a step of foresight. Redevelopment programs are making it possible for some family dwellings to replace outworn tenements. Whether or not families increase or there continues the present pattern of high percentage of nonfamily residents, people are in the inner city by the millions. With population forecasts that more and more people will be living in metropolitan regions in the future, it should be evident that the local church will do well to consider what it might do as part of a ministry in the inner city.

An inner city strategy for inner city ministry might be somewhat as follows:

1. Stop wailing guiltily for past neglect—the major amount of which was not realized as neglect by evangelicals until recently, at least by the majority of laymen. The Christians of inner city and suburbs alike should acknowledge that they do have a responsibility to both inner city and suburb. God calls the evangelicals by the Holy Spirit to be active in the inner city, in a new and urgent sense, in the light of the present crises.

2. No church should move out of the inner city without previous thought and planning about how to serve the people who might be left there. In some cases there is no ministry

possible due to the exodus of people to make way for highways, industrial plants or other depopulating events. Perhaps the church has tried to reach what few people are left and have met with no success. On the other hand, there may be many people to be ministered to. In this case, the church should always assess whether or not it can launch a community ministry to those around it. If it believes it can, it should launch such a ministry when conditions favorable to it include the necessary requirements enumerated earlier in the chapter. Either the church should stay to operate it or enable inner city evangelicals to operate it, having left them there for that purpose.

3. Suburban churches should form quasi-mission boards, referred to in this way because they may be called mission boards or by some other name, as long as they do the real work of missionary arms of the church. These boards might well be composed of personnel from one or several sources. The board in one instance might be from the one church that is interested in the project and there may be no need for more members. Or there might be a board with representatives of churches of one of the denominations within the vicinity of the city in question. They might be from several evangelical churches of several denominational and undenominational affiliations within that metropolitan area. These churches and the mission boards they organize should collaborate in operating branch churches or mission stations. Such operations should include evangelicals from the sections of the inner city areas in which they plan to operate, in both the planning and the carrying out of the project where it is possible to secure such participation. Such mission stations or branch churches might be in operation where churches had formerly held forth or might be in new locations as needed.

4. Included where possible, at or in connection with these operations, should be community and social service ministries as need for them is evident. At or separate from these locations

should be more evangelical Christian social agencies to do special work in the communities, directing people to the churches or mission stations. The practice of these agencies must be for all people of all kinds, and not only for those of the same religious identification as that of the sponsors.

5. Professional and supporting workers should be trained to meet special needs of the neighborhoods in which these inner city testimonies are located. Special need is for community organizers and intergroup relations specialists.

6. Let not prayer for revival and spiritual awakening be neglected. The inner city beachhead is an ideal spot to receive a visitation of God's power.[7] What if we lament that people in the inner city are too transient, their families broken up, they have no money to support a church? Might these not be prerequisites for affluent Christians doing something instead of nothing? The early churches under the apostles and their successors began and flourished in the cities, and were composed of people of all kinds, including the poor. Nothing is too hard for God.

7. Plans and methods used should be flexible in case of social change in the inner city, including social mobility patterns.

Recruitment for a Calling

We haven't said much about the kind of workers we have been taking for granted who will do all the work we have said needs doing. We should note that it has always been the responsibility of the individual group of believers to consider prayerfully which people are to be set aside for various gospel ministries. Workers in the cities are no different from Christian workers anywhere else except in some aspects of their ministrations. The church should not omit the search for workers for such areas as well as for others.

One aspect of the church's strategy today is going to have to be to recruit more workers to be pastors, missionaries, inner city workers, Christian social service staff, and many more personnel in helping professions and occupations.

It is no doubt thought by many that scientific and secularizing forces have turned the attention of Christian young people from the traditional ministerial paths, with the lure of larger incomes in search of higher status and the acquisition of more material possessions. Other factors are of equal or greater significance, since lures of the above-mentioned kind have always been present in the centuries of the Church's experience.

First, we have told our youth that the pastorate and missionary service are *full-time service* in a sense in which other helping vocations like medicine are not. It is true that the Lord does set aside certain persons by His call for special ministries. Yet we should assure our youth that whatever their field they too are included in our praying "the Lord of the harvest" to "send forth labourers into his harvest." [8] In the face of present social crises, we ought to make more emphasis on the need there is in special Christian social service ministries in which Christian professionals can be used as full-time workers.

Second, our youth are seeing the need of dealing with the great social problems of the day. By way of all mass media of communication as well as by personal experience and observation, they are stirred to do something about them. They are volunteering for the helping professions in great numbers. The ministry, which once had the highest status in the American community, is thought of as but one of several helping professions. It used to be that, with the scarcity of doctors and lawyers and teachers, the minister was the one person with any considerable amount of education in many communities, and was thought of as the one who could deal with the social problems of the day as well as with the spiritual ones. When young people wanted to volunteer for careers in coping with many problems now dealt with by social workers, psychologists, teachers, they volunteered for the ministry.

Today, as social problems increase, young people are asking the churches and colleges and seminaries, "Why aren't you preparing people to deal with delinquency, child abuse, narcotics use, problems of the mentally retarded, and the like?"

Again we have to repeat the theme that it is not an either/or but a both/and matter. We need to regard all preparation for any Christian's life and work as preparation in one sense for full-time Christian service. In another very urgent sense, we need to re-emphasize the need for servants of God to prepare for the full-time work of the pastorate (teaching pastors [9]) and other church-related callings so vital to the churches. In these days, some *part-time* pastors are reaching people with the gospel which they could not afford to do if they did not hold another job on the side to provide support for their families. In this way they can minister to people who cannot pay them enough to prevent them from holding another position. Such pastors and Christian workers also need training.

References for Chapter 20

1. Matthew 13:38.
2. Acts 6:1–6; 1 Timothy 3:8–13.
3. Oscar E. Feucht (ed.), *Helping Families Through the Church* (St. Louis, Concordia Publishing House, 1957), Chapter 8.
4. Alan Keith-Lucas, *The Church and Social Welfare* (Philadelphia, Westminster Press, 1962).
5. Southern Baptist Convention, "Church Community Weekday Ministries," current *pamphlet*.
6. Romans 12:13.
7. 2 Chronicles 7:14.
8. Matthew 9:38.
9. Ephesians 4:11.

21

Christian Personal Responsibility for Social Action

Personal Involvement

From the subject of a church's community responsibilities it is but a step to the climax point of our study—the individual Christian and his personal responsibility.

We have been contending that the Christian does the most basic work of all when he leads a soul to Christ, because that changed life in so many ways makes its own impact on society. We have asserted that the Christian engages in appropriate social action when clearly led to do so. We have seen these factors as two sides of the one coin of alertness to personal responsibility for the needs of others, and not as two opposites.

J. A. Witmer, writing in *Bibliotheca Sacra,* gives succinct expression to the truth of the Christian's social responsibility, after he had cited scriptural bases for it:

A Christian legitimately can participate in social reform activities. A Christian should be interested in securing clean, honest, efficient government from the local up to the national level. The Christian should be concerned with reduction of gambling and vice in his locality to a minimum . . . a Christian legitimately can share in such philanthropic activities as the Red Cross and his local Community Chest. Participation in this type of endeavor affords many opportunities for Christian witness to the alert believer. And yet the Christian must recognize that his responsibilities to participate in these activities (do) not spring ultimately from his membership in the society of Christians but from his place in human society. Therefore, . . . participation in such activities must be the object of prayerful pondering and individual direction from the Lord. Here again Christian love must prevail among brethren in Christ, recognizing that in such matters the Lord leads each individual differently. The application of these principles of Christian social responsibility to modern situations and problems requires unusual spiritual discernment and a constant, sensitive response to the guidance of the Lord. The ever-present danger is to become enmeshed in worthwhile secondary activities to the neglect of primary responsibilities as a Christian. However, properly subordinated and correlated to the primary ministry of proclaiming the gospel and winning individual souls to a saving knowledge of Christ, such activities of a humanitarian character can be wonderfully used and honored of God. Paul expressed the principle involved when he wrote concerning his own activities, "I am made all things to all men, that I might by all means save some" (1 Corinthians 9:22).[1]

Witmer was writing before the sixties, when evangelicals seemed to think of social responsibility as a real part of the Christian total responsibility, but as a kind of small appendage or minor adjunct. The exploding social problems of the sixties have changed all that, and it is now more in proportion to refer to preaching the gospel and dealing with social problems as complementary parts of one ministry and inseparable rather than as primary and secondary. But, remember: The gospel must always be given when possible whether or not there is any opportunity to give other aid.

The Christian does not content himself to adjust his conduct according to the changing social climate of his own day. Always a citizen of two worlds, of this world as well as of Heaven, he asks, "What did Jesus do?" He knows that what Jesus did and said contains principles valid in any age.

At the risk of oversimplification, we offer three propositions based upon what Jesus did and said and what we may infer therefrom that the individual Christian may do:

1. During Jesus' ministry He did not initiate any major social reforms in the sense in which we usually use that term. Therefore, if Christians do become instrumental in bringing about major social reforms, they do so as God leads them in their own personal mission on earth and not as a divine mandate for all. (Whether Jesus would do differently now in a democratic society instead of what He did in the nondemocratic society in which He lived is an interesting question. The fact is that He did not do differently from what the Scriptures relate.)

2. Jesus did minister to the basic human needs of man as well as to the spiritual ones. An outstanding example is His feeding of the five thousand. He also specified that He leaves it to us to do good to the poor who are always around to be helped.[2]

3. How much the individual Christian may be able to discharge the scriptural mandate to be of service to those in need will be as the Holy Spirit enlightens the mind through the Scriptures and clear providential circumstances. It is helpful to note that we are simply to be ready to give individual or group help to people as they show need, spiritual or material or both, as God makes it possible to give.

It is helpful to note the intertwining of social and spiritual concerns in Jesus' feeding the multitudes. While our Lord was concerned for the physical needs of the people, he rebuked many of those he fed for not putting spiritual matters first.[3] This is not to imply that we require spiritual acquiescence or even mere verbal compliance to our doctrinal positions before we give needed material help. Jesus did not. It does serve to show that Jesus never lost sight of spiritual values.

Two comments remain to complete our summary of the Christian's personal responsibility for social action:

1. Responsibility lies with Christians also to bring about *systems change,* as much as other people are responsible. If

the Christian has it in his power to help anyone without reference to such helping as consciously effectuating major change, he should do the deed of mercy for its own value and for Jesus' sake. But if he has it in his power to go beyond that and implement great changes in the present system of production and delivery of food to the hungry so they need not continue any longer in hunger, this and other major adjustments are the imperatives at the root of today's social crises, as we have seen.

2. Looking from the macroscopic big change to the microscopic, we note that social responsibility evidenced in Christian social action includes God's awareness of *each act* the Christian does.[4] There is in sociology the term *social act* which refers to the smallest unit of social life. Alex Inkeles calls it "the true atom of social life."[5] Certainly Christians ought to be at least as concerned about the quality and significance of each individual act as are other people. If we are always insistent about examining every social action issue which might confront us, and are sure to scrutinize any proposed church-connected community service project, social act by social act, and all in the light of the Scriptures and the guidance of the Holy Spirit, we are not liable to go too far afield in our discharge of social responsibility.

The Christian and Political Action

We have suggested that social change should be brought about by the use of established channels—the vote, the ballot-box, the courts, legislative action. We have suggested courses of action, as on pages 89 and 90. If we agree that such should be done, and have it in our power to do so, yet refuse to use available channels when we should, we are no better than the oft-quoted mice in the fable. They all agreed the cat should have a bell around his neck so as to warn the mice of the cat's approach, but no mouse would agree to hang the bell on the cat.

Let us examine the question of the Christian in politics. We must first note that there is a reluctance on the part of many Americans to becoming personally involved in a political career. Yet, a fear entertained by some Christians not true of some others who assail politics is a fear that involvement would bring contamination. In the case of the Christian there is the additional wariness against corruption and dishonesty, and rightly so.

Let us offer the frank opinion that many Christians should be active in politics. (See pages 102 and 103.) For one thing, this would be, or should be, a way of procuring help for the poor. Doing this would call for looking further than we have done so far, to see the basis for engaging in this kind of social action.

Senator Mark O. Hatfield helps us view the issue. He says, in a reference to the local church and the individuals which make it up, and all these collectively as a power unit in society: "No amount of government legislation can replace the function of the church which is to change men's hearts by the power of Christ. The church has no other mission. It betrays its Lord when it seeks merely to act as a power bloc in the political arena. It falls short of its high calling when it serves only as another of the many community welfare organizations." [6] He repeats the primacy of spiritual change in his "two-fold challenge to the citizen Christian. First, it is to redeem the citizens of our society and thereby to build a better foundation for government. This can be done by obedience to the Great Commission, the teaching of the Gospel of Christ. The second challenge is to be willing to serve God in politics and government if that is where he wants you. The great experiment that is America calls to each generation for the kind of men and women who will dare to make this nation what it was meant to be." [7]

The Senator points out the secret of balance which can be

achieved in the Christian politician: "My relationship with Christ gives me a base—an absolute—both for my personal and my public life. . . . The dynamics of this relationship can give the Christian both an absolute foundation and the freedom to deal with the relativity of the political sphere. There is a perspective, an equilibrium, and a total world view which the Christian can achieve, and this gives him the capacity to deal with relative and changing circumstances." [8]

In a very incisive statement, Senator Hatfield relates the work of Christ in the world in this dispensation to the Christian through whom He works: "The responsibility of the public servant is not to Christianize the institutions of government, but to bring the influence of Christ to bear upon them." [9] From this pinpointing of the individual Christian's function we look to the larger scene in the words of the Senator: "We are engaged in a cosmic battle between the forces of good and the forces of evil. The Scriptures speak often of the conflict between good and evil within the human heart and soul and conscience. What we often forget is that this personal battle is translated into social battles in the community, into conflicts between classes, races, economic interest groups, and ultimately, into conflicts between nations." [10]

Having taken this important excursion into the specific field of politics, we return to the large universe of social action in all its multiplicity. Granted that the individual Christian may now feel able to ascertain how he should fit into social action concerns today, he might want a word about how to assess when and how much to take action on projects larger than those which might be small enough for him to handle as one individual. Perhaps these will help:

1. The Christian should involve himself in real and urgent

situations which it is clearly the business of the church and its members to do something about, providing they have ability and personnel to do the work.

2. The Christian should not succumb to the temptation to dabble in other issues which would not be of the nature of clear need and calling for immediate attention. Also, he should not manufacture or force crises simply to keep stirred up by a feeling that he must always be engaged in social action or be disobedient if he is not.

3. There are enough chronic social ills present and continuing, like poverty and the harm it does to the many poor, to give reason for ongoing action ministries between emergencies.

Missionary Responsibility

Christian social responsibility may be to the entire world or to the local community or to the nation. In all these, it is a missionary responsibility.

Evangelical Christians in the America of today are as much missionaries to our present generation and culture as any missionaries have ever been in lands and cultures quite foreign to them as they entered. The main difference is that we are still living in the land which has been made more pagan while we have watched.

In addition to being missionaries to people here all their lives, we need to see ourselves with new eyes as key missionaries to the thousands of newcomers God sends into this country each year. A true view of missions still includes getting the gospel to people anywhere in the world, but now adds the great responsibility of learning how to deal with the multitudes God sent and is sending to us. For instance, this writer remembers many years ago a group of evangelicals circularized him and others, asking that we protest against planeloads of Puerto Ricans being brought into this country. He not only did not protest, but then and since took advantage of opportunities of ministries to them and other Latin Americans for Christ.

It is much the same issue, whether we speak of migrant workers in New Jersey or Arizona, blacks from the South, or whites from Hungary or Czechoslovakia. God sends them to us to help in all ways within our power.

Our own nation is at least as spiritually needy as any foreign mission field, and should not be exempt from the same intensification of evangelization as in any mission field. It requires more intensive training in many methods and concepts, especially in the field of communications, some of which have not even yet been discovered or perfected. Some methods are beginning to be better known, including the use of social service methods in evangelical Christian social welfare operations. Added to the Christian's training in evangelization, the training of evangelical Christian social workers in capacities from volunteer to professional would increase the Christian total effectiveness on the home front. It would parallel the practice of giving intensive training to the foreign missionary candidate.

A Particular Appeal (an epilogue)

We have said that one purpose of this book is to urge formation of an evangelical strategy for America's evangelization.

Without trained workers, many of the most difficult aspects of this work cannot be attempted.

Without the workers presenting themselves as God raises them up, they cannot be trained.

Without adequate facilities, they cannot be well prepared.

Therefore:

Pray the Lord to continue raising up workers, and to provide means for all facets of the carrying out of His ministries.

Organize new Christian social agencies.

Update methods and operation of existing agencies.

Make the local church the key to community ministries wherever possible. Improve church benevolences and counseling ministries and provide Christian social work personnel.

See that all workers are trained in the Scriptures.

As an attempt to assist the above implementation, this book has sought to give a kind of orientation to the field of social action to aid the Christian's knowledge and use of it. Much information has been offered, howbeit partial, limited, opinionated. The author would welcome comments and suggestions so as to aid his own understanding and improve it.

The student should make his own as many of the ideas as will truly help him evaluate the many social issues of our day and his part in them. Giving advance thought to these matters often comes into helpful use and sometimes on short notice.

We have suggested some specific methods to use in coping with social problems. In other instances we have refrained from doing so, pending development of more satisfactory ways of solving them. Among some of the procedures we have suggested are: Education for Christian social service ministries; church and individual procedures for handling emergency social problems arising on short notice; recruitment of youth; local church ministries to community needs; and the conducting of inner city ministries. We have highlighted individual and group and societal action toward the needed change of social system malfunctions for the better by planned social change. We have urged entrance of youth into helping professions of the ministry and social work, among others, and have encouraged Christian involvement in politics; all of these as the Lord leads the individual.

The challenge of the day is for each individual to be a man

of God according to the scriptural prescription, and to urge the local church to be what it ought to be, by the same standard.

In a day when demonstrators are pledging themselves to suffer privation, exposure, imprisonment, insults, and injuries as a result of actions they take, whether or not the cause is a just one, how can the Christian do less than take good action in a good cause? [11]

Remaining identified with Christ, representing Him among men, and delivering help to those in need as we collaborate with them to improve their lot, are all of the highest priority in our time.

References for Chapter 21

1. J. A. Witmer, "Christian Social Responsibility," *Bibliotheca Sacra* (January, 1953), Vol. 10, No. 437, pp. 218, 219.
2. Mark 14:7.
3. John 6:26–29.
4. 2 Corinthians 5:10; 1 Peter 1:17; Hebrews 4:12, 13.
5. Alex Inkeles, *What Is Sociology?* (Englewood Cliffs, New Jersey, Prentice-Hall, 1964), p. 25; also p. 70.
6. Mark O. Hatfield, "How Can a Christian Be in Politics?" in Clouse, et al., *Protest and Politics*, p. 18.
7. *Ibid.*, pp. 15, 16.
8. *Ibid.*, p. 17.
9. *Ibid.*, p. 18.
10. *Ibid.*, p. 13.
11. Galatians 4:18.

Bibliography

The Bible

The Declaration of Independence of the United States of America

The Constitution of the United States of America

The Encyclopedia of Social Work (1965)

Bell, Daniel (ed.), *The Radical Right,* Garden City, New York, Doubleday, Anchor Books (paperback), 1963

Berger, Peter L., *Invitation to Sociology,* Garden City, New York, Doubleday, Anchor Books (paperback), 1963

Bertrand, Alvin, *Basic Sociology,* New York, Appleton-Century-Crofts, 1967

Bredemeier, Harry C., and Toby, Jackson, *Social Problems in America,* New York, John Wiley and Sons, Inc., 1960

Bredemeier, Harry C., and Stephenson, Richard M., *The Analysis of Social Systems,* New York, Holt, Rinehart and Winston, Inc., 1965

Buswell, James O., III, *Slavery, Segregation and the Scriptures,* Grand Rapids, Wm. B. Eerdmans Publishing Co., 1954

Cairns, Earle E., *Saints and Society,* Chicago, Moody Press, 1960

Caplovitz, David, *The Poor Pay More,* New York, The Free Press, 1963

Catherwood, H. F. R., *The Christian in Industrial Society,* London, the Tyndale Press (paperback), 1966

Cohen, Nathan E. (ed.), *Social Work and Social Problems,* New York, National Association of Social Workers (paperback), 1964

Cox, Harvey, *The Secular City,* New York, The Macmillan Co. (paperback), 1965

Clouse, Robert G., Linder; Robert D., and Pierard, Richard V., *Protest and Politics,* Greenwood, S.C., The Attic Press, 1968

Davis, Kenneth S. (ed.), *The Paradox of Poverty in America,* New York, The H. W. Wilson Co., 1969

Davis, Kingsley, *Human Society,* New York, Macmillan Co., 1949

247

DeRemer, Bernard R., *Moody Bible Institute: A Pictorial History*, Chicago, Moody Press, 1960

Duhl, Leonard J. (ed.), *The Urban Condition*, New York, Basic Books, 1963

Faulkner, Harold U., and Kepner, Tyler, *America, Its History and People*, New York, Harper and Brothers, 1947

Ferman, Louis A., Kornbluh, Joyce L., and Haber, Alan, *Poverty in America*, Ann Arbor, University of Michigan Press, 1965

Feucht, Oscar E., *Helping Families Through the Church*, St. Louis, Concordia Publishing House, 1957

Fink, Arthur E., Anderson, C. Wilson, and Conover, Merrill B., *The Field of Social Work*, New York, Holt, Rinehart and Winston, Inc., fifth edition, 1968

Fletcher, Joseph, *Situation Ethics*, Philadelphia, Westminster Press, 1966

Franklin, John Hope, *From Slavery to Freedom*, New York, Vintage Books (paperback), 1967

Freedman, Leonard, and Cotter, Cornelius P. (eds.), *Issues of the Sixties*, Belmont, Calif., Wadsworth Publishing Co., Inc. (paperback), 1961

Graham, Billy, *World Aflame*, Garden City, Doubleday and Co., Inc., 1965

Hamilton, Gordon, *The Theory and Practice of Social Casework*, New York, Columbia University Press, 1951

Handlin, Oscar, *Fire-bell in the Night*, Boston, Little, Brown and Co., 1964

Haselden, Kyle, *Mandate for White Christians*, Richmond, Virginia, John Knox Press, 1966

Heilbroner, Robert L., *The Making of Economic Society*, Englewood Cliffs, N.J., Prentice-Hall, 1962

Henry, Carl F. H., *Aspects of Christian Social Ethics*, Grand Rapids, Wm. B. Eerdmans, 1964

Henry, Carl F. H., *The Uneasy Conscience of Modern Fundamentalism*, Grand Rapids, Wm. B. Eerdmans Publishing Co., 1947

Hofstadter, Richard, *The Age of Reform*, New York, Vintage Books (paperback), 1955

Hofstadter, Richard, *Social Darwinism in American Thought*, Boston, The Beacon Press, revised (paperback), 1955

Homans, George C., *The Human Group*, New York, Harcourt, Brace and Co., 1950

Hopkins, Charles H., *The Rise of the Social Gospel in American Protestantism*, New Haven, Yale University Press, 1940

Horton, Paul B., and Leslie, Gerald R., *The Sociology of Social Problems*, New York, Appleton-Century-Crofts, third edition, 1965

Inkeles, Alex, *What Is Sociology?* Englewood Cliffs, N.J., Prentice-Hall, 1964

Keith-Lucas, Alan, *The Church and Social Welfare*, Philadelphia, Westminster Press (paperback), 1962

King, Martin Luther, *Why We Can't Wait*, New York, Harper & Row, Publishers, 1963

Lippitt, Ronald, Watson, Jeanne, and Westley, Bruce, *The Dynamics of Planned Change*, New York, Harcourt, Brace and World, 1958

Mathews, Shailer, *The Social Gospel*, Philadelphia, The Griffith and Rowland Press, 1910

McKenna, David (ed.), *The Urban Crisis*, Grand Rapids, Zondervan Publishing House, 1969

Meissner, Hanna H. (ed.), *Poverty in the Affluent Society*, New York, Harper & Row, Publishers (paperback), 1966

Merton, Robert K., and Nisbet, Robert A., *Contemporary Social Problems*, New York, Harcourt, Brace and World, second edition, 1966

Moberg, David O., *Inasmuch: Christian Social Responsibility in the Twentieth Century*, Grand Rapids, Wm. B. Eerdmans Publishing Co. (paperback), 1965

Morison, Samuel, *The Oxford History of the American People*, New York, the Oxford University Press, 1965

National Advisory Commission on Civil Disorders, *Report*, New York, Bantam Books (paperback), 1968

Ogburn, William F., and Nimkoff, Meyer F., *Sociology*, Boston, Houghton, Mifflin Co., 1964

Pannell, William E., *My Friend the Enemy*, Waco, Texas, Word Books, 1968

Peterson, Houston (ed.), *A Treasury of the World's Great Speeches*, New York, Simon and Schuster, 1954

Pumphrey, Ralph E., and Pumphrey, Muriel W., *The Heritage of American Social Work*, New York, Columbia University Press (paperback), 1961

Riesman, David, Glaser, Nathan, and Denney, Reuel, *The Lonely Crowd*, Garden City, Doubleday and Co., Inc., Anchor Books (paperback), 1953

Romanyshyn, John M., *Social Welfare: Charity to Justice,* New York, Random House and Council on Social Work Education, 1971

Rose, Arnold M., *Sociology,* New York, Alfred A. Knopf, Inc., 1965

Schapiro, J. Salwyn, *Liberalism and the Challenge of Fascism,* New York, Octagon Books, Inc., 1964

Seligman, Ben B. (ed.), *Poverty as a Public Issue,* New York, The Free Press (paperback), 1965

Skinner, Tom, *Black and Free,* Grand Rapids, Zondervan Publishing House, 1968

Smelser, Neil J., and Smelser, William T. (eds.), *Personality and Social Systems,* New York, John Wiley & Sons, Inc., 1964

Smith, Timothy L., *Revivalism and Social Reform,* New York, Abingdon Press, 1951

Towle, Charlotte, *Common Human Needs,* New York, National Association of Social Workers, 1945, revised (paperback), 1965

Vasey, Wayne, *Government and Social Welfare,* New York, Holt, Rinehart and Winston, 1958

Wilensky, Harold L., and Lebeaux, Charles N., *Industrial Society and Social Welfare,* Russell Sage Foundation, 1958 and 1965 (in the first Free Press paperback edition), 1965

Wirt, Sherwood E., *The Social Conscience of the Evangelical,* Harper & Row, Publishers, New York, 1968

Yinger, J. Milton, *Sociology Looks at Religion,* New York, Macmillan Co. (paperback), 1961

Young, Whitney M., *To Be Equal,* New York, McGraw-Hill Book Co., 1964

Index